MW01633490

Advance praise for

MAKE ROOM
for Happiness and Intimacy

"Healthy communication is to a relationship what blood is to the body—essential. When we are 'in love' communication seems so easy. Why does it become difficult after marriage? Dr. Jeff Rees not only answers that question, but offers practical help in how to move from destructive communication to healthy communication. Anyone in a serious relationship will find this book most helpful."

—GARY CHAPMAN, PHD
author of *The Five Love Languages*

"A good, happy marriage is foundational for our lives. Choosing a good spouse is important, yet learning how to communicate and deal with issues as 'two become one' is challenging! *Make Room* gives helpful insights gained from years of counseling and a variety of real life experiences. I hope you smile, and sometimes grimace, as you see yourself in these Case Studies and learn how to be a better communicator, which leads to a better love-filled relationship."

—DAVID WEEKLEY
founder and Chairman David Weekley Homes

"Building a great marriage is both God-honoring and personally rewarding. However, this building process is not without challenges. In *Make Room,* Jeff Rees provides a blueprint for navigating these challenges and for strengthening even the best marriages."

—CARA AND LANCE BERKMAN
six-time MLB All-Star

"Jeff Rees's concept of a couple's future home resonates, and it puts him in the category of elite teacher and coach. Good coaching is about putting passionate players in position to make plays. *Make Room* goes deep and clears the path for JOY; the eternal other that has no opposite. Read it and score!"

—Spencer Tillman
network broadcaster, husband, author, and leadership expert

"*Make Room* is a simple and helpful tool to encourage couple intimacy through the development of meaningful communication. Dr. Rees creates an excellent visual guide to understanding and discovering your partner."

—Cynthia M. Barkley, LPC-S

"*Make Room* is a great book for married couples but also for those planning to marry. Jeff Rees's emphasis on communication highlights the importance of empathy. To be a good communicator one must be an empathetic listener."

—Robert C. McNair
business leader and owner of the NFL's Houston Texans

"Marriage is a complicated and complex relationship to say the least. That's why so many never make it to the finish line and fail to discover true joy and fulfillment. *Make Room* gives practical advice for life together and offers valuable tools for relational success."

—Gregg Matte
pastor, speaker, and author of
Birds and Bees: A Conversation about God, Sex, and Sexuality

"Jeff Rees takes a unique approach in guiding couples to reach deeper levels of communication and self-discovery. This is an excellent resource for engaged and married couples to take the next step of 'knowing' one another. *Make Room* will be a resource I will often utilize and highly recommend to clients." —LAURA BRAZIEL, LPC, MFT

"*Make Room* is very personable, understandable, and engaging. The metaphor of the different rooms representing areas we should explore within marriage is intriguing, very relevant, and useful. Major kudos!"

—ANGELA M. PFEIFFER, PHD, LPC

"Jeff Rees has created a wonderful, easy to read, easy to follow guide for married couples and those considering marriage. I highly recommend it to anyone."

—MIKE MCGRAW
three-time NCAA National Championship golf coach

"Jeff Rees gives us creative and helpful tools to improve our communication in marriage. These will work for engaged couples, for newlyweds, and for those of us who've been married a long time. If you want to open the channels of heart-felt communication with your mate, read *Make Room*!"

—DAVID & DENISE GLENN
founders, Kardo International Ministries
(MotherWise/FatherWise Ministries) kardo.org

"All couples experience great chemistry when they begin but at some point there is a break in the chemistry. Whenever the break comes, couples are forced to make a decision as to what they will do to respond to this break. *Make Room* is a great tool in assessing what our rebuilding needs are. I plan to make it assigned reading to all newlyweds and those seeking counseling assistance." —MATT BARNHILL MA, CART

"Our good friend Jeff Rees has done the marriage education world a great service with this book. With creativity, practical case study examples, and excellent questions on significant life topics, couples have the opportunity to dig deep into conversations that matter. We will be making *Make Room* available to our couples that truly want to experience the highest levels of intimacy in their marriages."

—Brett and Kellie Hurst
Home Encouragement
homeencouragement.org

"Whether you are just beginning your marriage or have been at it a long time, *Make Room* will give you fresh methods for improving your marital health. *Make Room* will be a great template for those who do marriage counseling as well as for couples that want to do their own study. Dr. Rees did us all a favor in writing this book. Now go apply it to your life!"

—Roger Wernette
Executive Director, The Gathering of Men–Houston, and author of *Invited* and *Wholehearted*

"Really . . . another book on marriage? Hasn't the subject been covered already by countless numbers of authors? What is there left to say? I confess these were some of my thoughts when I received an early copy for my review. It didn't take long before I realized that this book is so unique in style and content. There is freshness and wisdom in Jeff Rees's insight, even (and especially) for those of us who have been married for decades. His emphasis upon communicating with your spouse is fantastic. Claudia and I highly recommend this book."

—Bob Mitchell
former president of Young Life
(and husband to Claudia since 1954)

MAKE ROOM

MAKE ROOM
FOR HAPPINESS & INTIMACY

Helping Couples Experience Meaningful Communication

Dr. Jeffrey W. Rees

Jeff Rees

Whitecaps Media
Houston

Whitecaps Media
Houston, Texas
whitecapsmedia.com

Make Room

ISBN: 978-1-942732-03-7

FIRST EDITION

Printed in the United States of America

To contact Jeff Rees to speak to your group or for information on bulk sales, please visit our website or email us at ran@whitecapsmedia.com

TABLE OF CONTENTS

	Introduction	1
1	Meaningful Communication	7
2	Construction Tools	15
3	The Blueprint	29
4	Formal Room	39
5	Living Room	51
6	Kitchen and Laundry Room	77
7	Office	91
8	Children's Room	97
9	Bathroom	105
10	Bedroom	117
11	Attic	127
12	Back Porch	133
13	The Home's Foundation	143
	Questions for Small Groups	153

To Martha—
for the journey we have shared
and the journey that awaits us,
I'm so glad we made room

HEY, I NEED
TO TALK TO
YOU.
OH NO,
NOT
AGAIN.

Introduction

I have talked to hundreds of couples about all kinds of marriage challenges. By the time my involvement is requested the initial problem has gone from molehill to mountain. The situation is cancerous. The couple is no longer trying to solve a single problem. They are just trying to stay together. Words have become weapons. Screams are heard in the silence. I sit with these couples and hear their heartbreaking comments:

> "I can't believe I married the wrong person."
>
> "We had a great honeymoon six years ago, but it has been downhill ever since."
>
> "I feel like I am in prison, and the key has been thrown away."

> "On my wedding day I wish some brave person would have questioned my decision. With the slightest bit of encouragement, I would not have walked down that aisle. It was the biggest mistake of my life."

> "I used to hate my marriage, but things have gotten worse. I don't hate anymore—I don't even feel anymore."

There are times I help facilitate healing and see these marriages restored. There are times when that is not the case.

I believe in unconditional love. Unconditional love is indispensable and desperately needed in keeping relationships healthy and happy. Usually, when we mention unconditional love we are talking about loving those who have wounded us.

Our partners have caused us pain, but we love them anyway. We choose to love in spite of the hurt. We choose to love though offended and mistreated. We choose to love without requiring our partner to make us feel better or even apologize. We choose to love without condition. Every person should love unconditionally at some point. We are fortunate when we are recipients of it.

We regularly call upon unconditional love to keep the peace when angry words are hurled. We bite our lips and endure. We take a deep breath, give grace, and hope things will improve. However, it is best when we love fully and freely *without* disappointment, *without* pain, and *without* struggle. No one desires to live in a relationship where love is hard to give and harder to receive. We all want to be in a relationship where love is present and active, where love supports our living.

Loving and living are connected.

When I help my wife live well, it is an expression of love. The number of material things we possess and the forms of luxury we enjoy do not define "living well." These things only provide temporary pleasure. They do not sustain or foster true love. Love thrives through happiness and intimacy with one another. Happiness produces contentment, and intimacy creates unity. *Loving and living are connected.*

My wife's journey through life will include loss, opportunity, and an assortment of challenges. She will play many roles: daughter, wife, mother, sibling, teacher, mentor, neighbor, employee, supervisor, friend, and grandmother. She will savor the sweetness of success and taste the bitterness of failure. She will experience demands, disappointments, and occasional tragedies. There will be health crises and faith battles. She will experience adventure and wonder. She will age beautifully, each year turning like the pages of an enchanting novel. In other words, she will live. As her life partner, it is my joy to love her in those spaces and places; in those tunnels, turns, and detours along the journey. *Loving and living are connected.*

My objective in writing this book is to help couples in their communication skills. I am still a student learning how to love better and deeper. I am making better grades each semester. I've moved from Fail to Pass and I am on my way to the dean's list. I've learned that my achievements and successes in loving well are directly proportionate in how well I "make room." When someone asks me how to have a closer relationship with his or her spouse my response is one word: "Move." We are all capable of moving. There is an art in learning how to *move closer.*

For over thirty years I have provided premarital counseling to couples. I offer a visual concept of the couple's future home. Each room represents a way of living. Couples walk through each room together in order to discover and discern how each of them wants to live. In this discovery process they ask themselves, "How can I help my partner live well?" Understanding how your mate wants to live helps you better understand the ways you can express love. We love each other well by helping each other live well.

Couples that have participated in this exercise with me have asked me to put the process in writing. While writing the material, I expanded and modified the exercise so married couples would also benefit. I hope that happiness and intimacy are deepened and magnified for you and yours as each of you "make room."

In our exercise we use a house as a metaphor for life and living, and we walk through certain rooms of the house. Each room represents a particular aspect of how we live. Beginning in chapter 4, you will begin your own walk through the house, and in each room you will find case studies followed by questions that speak about real issues. The case studies are layered with many philosophical dynamics, views, and possibilities. But before we begin the exercise, we'll go over the building tools and blueprints to aid in the construction of your "house." Couples are encouraged to use these tools and blueprints as they review the case studies and questions and share their perspectives and assessments. The aim of this exercise is for couples to discover, connect, embrace, learn, and support each other in deeper ways than before. The last chapter, the home's foundation, is *crucial* to the entire house and binds the structure of the home together.

Many couples have embraced this exercise and increased their ability to communicate and to foster greater trust, appreciation, and intimacy. I hope that for you as well.

Dr. Jeffrey W. Rees

ONE

Meaningful Communication

I was talking with a young couple several weeks prior to their wedding day. They were a sweet couple, likable and engaging. It was no surprise they were attracted to each other. Both were first-born children coming from supportive, healthy homes. They were friendly and open to me even though I was fifteen years their senior.

The idea of their dream home surfaced as we talked. Bob said, "I want a home that resembles the heart of the Texas Hill Country. I love that look." The young bride-to-be dropped her jaw as if her name was just announced on *The Price is Right*. "I love that look, too! How perfect!" Her response was just shy of a squeal. Caroline looked at me and said, "We were made for each other. We like the same things and feel the same way about everything!"

As she grinned from ear-to-ear, I commented, "Well, a few different images come to mind when I think of a Texas Hill Country home. What are you thinking, Bob?" Bob said, "I'm a simple kind of guy. I want a rustic exterior with faded gray wood planks, antique furnishings, a rusty barbed-wire fence that circles the house, and a tin-roofed barn behind the house, and it would be great if that barn leaned just a little bit. To top it off, it would have patches of wild bluebonnet flowers around the homestead. Oh, and a golden retriever sitting on the front porch!"

Caroline's smile completely vanished. Her *Price-is-Right* enthusiasm totally evaporated. "Barbed-wire?" She almost choked on the word. "And you know I'm leery of big dogs. I like cats." With that statement, Bob's face contorted a bit.

She continued, "I was thinking big limestone blocks with polished high-gloss woods and wrought-iron chandeliers, which would match the exterior gas lanterns. Haven't you ever been to Barton Creek?" Bob's contorted face stayed frozen throughout her description. She lost him once she uttered the "C-word." Caroline then turns to me to continue the conversation. Bob takes a step behind Caroline where she can't see him and mouths to me, "CAT? NO WAY."

But wait; didn't they both love the idea of having a Texas Hill Country home a few minutes before? Now they were standing in front of me with nervous laughter and fidgety postures. It was an uncomfortable moment. The couple still loved each other. That hadn't changed. They would still marry in a few weeks, but at that moment each seemed a little embarrassed and perturbed with the other. Is this a preview of conversations to come during married life? Will conversations of frustration and disillusionment be predictable and regular?

In the 1967 film, *Cool Hand Luke*, Paul Newman's character, Luke, is a prisoner who will not submit to the system of the prison camp. Luke attempts to escape, but is eventually captured and returned to camp. The warden has Luke's legs shackled, telling him that it is for his own good. Luke sarcastically retorts, "I wish you would stop being so good to me, Cap'n." The warden responds by striking Luke with a leather strap. As Luke falls to the ground, the warden faces the other prisoners watching the exchange and voices the classic line, "What we've got here is failure to communicate."[1]

How many marriages reflect similar circumstances? How many husbands or wives feel they are in prison and want to escape? Some feel they are in shackles. Some feel the sting of their partners' words like a leather strap across the face. Many couples say that the most significant issue

---

[1] *Cool Hand Luke*, directed by Stuart Rosenberg, 1967, Jalem Productions.

in the relationship is the inability to communicate well with each other.

Where there is breakdown in communication, all kinds of other breakdowns will follow. It is a certainty. Frustration swells and anger grows. Unhealthy tension becomes an unwanted boarder. Awkward moments can turn into angry moments, and angry moments create wounds and leave scars. Couples begin to question their love for each other. "What we've got here is failure to communicate."

Communication is key to every relationship. If couples communicated better there would be less tension with personal finances. Physical intimacy would increase in both pleasure and frequency. The practice of training and disciplining children would be an expression of parental unity. However, too often couples do not engage in meaningful communication. It is important to note that it is not communication that is key to a healthy relationship—it is *meaningful* communication. You want communication with your spouse to be full of meaning, a kind of meaning that is fulfilling, satisfying, and helpful. Some people think talking is communicating. This is a grave mistake. Meaningful communication is not simply putting words on record, staking claim, or controlling position. Meaningful communication informs and reveals. It reduces fear and anxiety. It comforts, directs, and empowers. It is not my goal to enhance your negotiating skills or debating abilities. This book offers couples tools and guidance for meaningful communication to enhance clarity and understanding. Where there is lack of clarity and understanding, we assume. Assumptions create problems.

On a personal note

Here is an example in my own marriage. Through the years my wife Martha and I have been in large crowds. It could be the fairgrounds, the Houston Livestock Show and Rodeo, or the mall area of a large complex such as a concert hall or professional sports stadium. We realize we need to get to our seats, concession area, or maybe find a restroom. We stand in the midst of hundreds of people going nowhere fast. I suddenly possess this Dudley Do-Right surge of energy and exhibit a "here-I-come-to-save-the-day" attitude. I seize my wife by the hand and plow through the crowd. In my mind, I'm the deliverer. In my mind, I have led her through troubled waters. We arrive safely at our destination, and I have demonstrated once again that I'm her knight in shining armor. I never push people, and I never shove anyone aside, but I am steady and strong in my pursuit. And I always provide for her. There is no crowd I cannot conquer. She must be tickled pink.

One day she said, "I wish you wouldn't drag me through the crowd. I hate it." We had been married for over twenty years when she voiced this. I was stunned. All these years I had envisioned this act of leading her through crowds as helpful—even heroic. She, on the other hand, felt tugged, tired, and slightly tortured.

"What we've got here is failure to communicate."

The principles of this book provide a way to uncover and correct common communication glitches that hinder meaningful conversation. What you desire is intimate connection of the heart. By connecting to the heart of the one you love, you have a framework to compliment your partner's passions and support his or her aspirations.

TWO
Construction Tools

Construction (kun-struk-shun) n. The act, process, or business of building. It is an important concept about your relationship. You need to think of yourself as a construction worker. You are a builder. You are shaping, crafting, and creating a life together. You are building your home. You are building your family. Your two lives are shared and joined in the most intimate of ways. You are constructing and creating a living partnership.

Build *well*.

Use the right *tools*.

Have you ever used the wrong tool in a building project? It is frustrating, at best, and potentially injurious. When couples use inappropriate tools of communication such as blame, silence, accusation, sarcasm, ridicule, threat, and other such instruments, frustration and wounds ensue. Some people use these destructive tools because they're all they know. These "tools" are easy to reach and easy to use because of our selfish natures. Sometimes these harsh tools can be effective in making a point, or enabling us to get our way, but they are more likely to bring emotional bruises and lasting damage to a relationship. There are better tools to use to experience meaningful communication.

Three Tools for Meaningful Communication

TOOL 1: PRACTICE EMPATHETIC LISTENING

In his book *The 7 Habits of Highly Effective People*, author Stephen Covey points out that we should first seek to understand before we seek to be understood.[1] But instead of seeking to understand a new thought or perspective, it is our nature to protect a position we already hold. We are inclined to filter information we receive based on our own life histories. Our personal views determine what is "appropriate" and "right" about a matter. When our personal views differ from our partners', a breeding ground for arguments and disagreements is created.

---

[1] Stephen R. Covey, *The 7 Habits of Highly Effective People* (New York, New York; Free Press, 2004), 239.

An empathetic listener *desires* to appreciate the other person's view and *seeks* to better understand how family heritage and values impacts his or her partner's perspectives. Empathetic listeners use their eyes and heart, not just their ears. The eyes and heart are where we make connection.

One way to gauge your empathetic listening posture is to observe how your response creates connection. Empathetic listening fuels connection, whereas other responses typically deflect, dilute, or diminish connection. For example, a friend confides in you and says, "My marriage is falling apart." You might try to help solve the problem, or counter with a response intended to be supportive. You are trying to be a good friend by saying things like:

> "My friend, there are other fish in the sea."
>
> "Well, there are no children involved. So that is a good thing."
>
> "You know, if your marriage ends in divorce, it will be their loss."

While well-intended and not necessarily bad, these responses don't acknowledge the pain your friend is experiencing. Empathy is not about problem solving, diluting the situation, or offering some kind of silver lining. It is about recognizing that your friend hurts because his or her marriage is falling apart. What your friend might need most is expressed *connection* and *care*. This is the goal of empathetic listening.

An empathetic response includes an open and welcoming body posture accompanied by words that express acknowledgement of the friend's feelings and appreciation for his or her friendship and trust. As an empathetic listener, you might respond to your friend by saying something like, "Wow. Those feelings must be so hard to deal with. Thank you for trusting me and sharing your pain with me. I am here for you and I care for you deeply."

You are a calm and engaging presence that communicates, "I am *with* you, and I am *for* you." An empathetic response conveys recognition and care for one's feelings and perspective.[2] Empathy creates and fuels *connection*. That's your standard of measure, and that is your goal. Nothing replaces connection.

Someone may ask, "But what if my partner's view is irrational or illogical?" We are best equipped to deal with irrational or illogical thinking during connection, not during disconnection. Empathetic listening has a way to speak to the heart of your mate. Expressed connection and care can actually guide your partner to new thoughts and help them consider a different perspective.

---

[2] Theresa Wiseman, "A concept analysis of empathy," *Journal of Advanced Nursing* (August 1996): 1162–67.

Bob and Caroline's initial exchange did not include empathetic listening. Their goal was not to fuel connection. Their goal was to fuel their own perspectives. They were more interested in their personal views of a Texas Hill Country home than learning about the views and desires of each other. This led to assumptions and misplaced conclusions, and the couple ended up bothered and discouraged. Now, let's be honest. Will all conversations be filled with empathy? No. But when you feel tension or distance with your partner, *move* toward empathetic listening. The issue becomes secondary while connection and care with your loved one becomes primary. Issues are best resolved through connection, not coercion.

We do not typically see our "assistance" or "advice" as coercion. We might sincerely be attempting to offer the best of help, but without connection our words come across as meddling, dominance, or even provocation.

On a personal note

I remember having a chance to go tubing with Martha on a beautiful summer's day while on vacation. We were each in separate tubes when she became trapped in the water's current. The water kept her circling in a bowl of riverbed boulders, and she was unable to break free from the current. I was able to pull myself to the side of the river and hold on to a branch to steady myself while I attempted to coach her on how to escape the current's grasp. My voice was raised so she could hear me over the sound of rushing water, and her anxiety level was rising in succession. My "yelling" was not helping the situation. I thought my instruction was clear and helpful. She did not. My best option was to walk upstream, come down the river again, and guide myself into the bowl with her. As I moved into the bowl, I embraced her. I assured her that we were all good and that we would work together to push ourselves out of the circular current. We succeeded without a great deal of drama or hardship. Our connection made all the difference. The issue or problem at hand has a much better chance of being resolved favorably with meaningful connection. In many instances, we must first connect, and then address the matter.

TOOL 2: CHOOSE DIALOGUE OVER DISCUSSION

Later in this book, I will present you with a variety of case studies and questions. The exercises are to create awareness, appreciation, understanding, and discovery. Therefore, do not "take sides" with the individuals in the case studies. If you take sides and try to force your partner to accept your view about a case study, the exercise will be less fruitful. To avoid taking sides, choose dialogue over discussion.[3] Dialogue is a great construction tool.

---

[3] Peter M. Senge, *The Fifth Discipline: The Art & Practice of the Learning Organization* (New York, New York; Doubleday/Currency, 1990), 240.

Remember how we talked about using the right tools to build? Many conversations at home always consist of discussion. Dialogue is the better tool.

The word *discussion* shares a root word (-*cuss*, meaning to beat or strike) with *percussion* and *concussion*. Discussion is used to "beat" people to our view and way of thinking. The object of discussion is to persuade and win people over to our understanding, or at least to our side. This beating does not need to be loud or demanding. Persuasion can be accomplished in a kind and gentle fashion. But note that persuasion is the goal of discussion. So, the person with the strongest voice, the person most unwilling to submit, the one most skilled in debate or negotiation, "wins." This happens in relationships all the time. If "beating" is a habitual practice, the "loser" of these discussions feels less valued over time. This leads to disengagement and distance in the relationship.

Dialogue comes from the Greek *dialogos*. *Dia* means "through" and *logos* means "word." When dialogue takes place each person expresses his or her "words" and *receives* the words of others. Dialogue asks each party to receive the other's "words" in an effort to understand. Dialogue does not imply agreement, but where there is dialogue there is no attempt to counter or to persuade. In all relationships there are certainly occasions when discussions are needed. Hopefully these discussions will not be harsh verbal beatings but merely necessary in order to make decisions through healthy forms of persuasion. However, the case studies in the book are not intended for discussion, but for dialogue. The objective is intimacy through discovery and understanding.

Dialogue fosters two great necessities for intimate conversation: transparency and open-mindedness.

Transparency. What does transparency mean in a relationship? It means that your mate can see beneath the exterior. By being transparent you help your partner understand what your thought processes are, what your motives are, and what makes you tick. Your partner needs to hear your convictions, hopes, dreams, and ideals, and understand why these dreams are important to you.

Open-mindedness. No one likes to think of himself or herself as narrow-minded. What we perceive to be acceptable, right, or normal is largely determined by our upbringing and value systems, not whether we are open- or close-minded.

When a person is fully transparent, allowing others to see beneath the exterior, he makes himself vulnerable. He is exposed. Therefore, transparency must be cultivated in an atmosphere of safety.

An open-minded person encourages others to be transparent and share their feelings without fear of reprisal. Deep, personal conversations with your partner will be compromised if there is any hint of judgment. Meaningful communication is limited if one feels compelled to walk a tightrope with their words.

Bob and Caroline's conversational breakdown finds healing with transparency and open-mindedness.

The next day Bob and Caroline take a walk in the park. Both are a little bothered by yesterday's exchange over the Texas Hill Country home. As they walk, Caroline realizes she lacks understanding. She feels led to show interest in his hopes and dreams and raises the subject once again. She asks in a soft, approaching tone, "Bob? I thought the description of your Texas Hill Country home was interesting. You usually like the look of new, as I do. So is there a faded, rustic, tin-roofed, rusty barbed-wire homestead that is calling your name?" She follows this question with a small inviting snicker. Her posture and comments communicate she is open-minded.

With that opening question Bob starts to walk in the warm waters of transparency. Caroline discovers that Bob's grandmother lived in a house very similar to Bob's description of his Texas Hill Country dream home. His grandmother died when Bob was eight. He fondly remembers her doting over him during the summer visits they made when she was alive. He adored running in the fields with his grandmother's big golden retriever, Max. With this insight, Caroline has a deeper appreciation for Bob's hopes and desires. She spontaneously feels a deeper connection with him. Both Bob and Caroline connect in a very meaningful way that afternoon. She sees things she didn't see before. This level of transparency is extremely important for couples. Transparency will only have its perfect result in a welcoming environment.

TOOL 3: EMBRACE THE UNIQUENESS AND BEAUTY OF YOUR RELATIONSHIP

I have been in hundreds of homes. In an attorney's home I visited he had converted the attic into his office. It was now a three-story house. The back wall of his office was all glass. It was a beautiful view. I've been in a few homes that had "secret passageways." I've been in homes that gave me great ideas about landscaping and maximizing space. I've been in a home that had the same floor plan as the home of a friend of mine. But I didn't recognize it; it had to be pointed out to me. The reason I didn't recognize it was because there were plenty of small differences throughout the home. The kitchen counter was a different material and contour. The windows were different shapes. The hearth of the fireplace was stone, not ceramic like my friend's.

Every house is different. One house has slate shingles, another has asphalt. One house has predominantly wood flooring, and another has Berber carpet. Just as each house is a unique mix of different colors, shapes, textures, tones, alterations, materials, exterior and interior features, so relationships are a distinct combination of characteristics. No house is the same, and no couple is the same.

Each couple has its own structure and material. Couples are different because each person contributes something different to the relationship. Unfortunately, some people don't see the uniqueness of their relationship as something to be celebrated, but something to be changed.

Now, some matters in your home need attention. If the roof leaks, repair it. If the carpet is worn, replace it. If you want to upgrade to custom kitchen cabinets, then do so. Changes to your house are ongoing, and changes (improvements) in your relationship will be ongoing. But celebrate and enjoy the place you call home. Celebrate and enjoy the uniqueness and beauty of *your* relationship.

Couples must learn to embrace their unique design and live in its beauty. Embrace the beauty of your one-of-a-kind relationship. Resistance to do so produces friction and instability. Learning to embrace your uniqueness will lead to greater stability and security as a couple.

On a personal note

I have always enjoyed athletic competition. Growing up I enjoyed athletic competition more than television viewing, playing board or video games, traveling, fishing, or anything else. I could not imagine a lifestyle without sports. As a young man, my hope was to play tennis, racquetball, basketball, golf, and softball as often as I could. I wanted to play until Jesus returned or my strength failed me—whichever came first. Early in our dating relationship, I discovered that my future wife, Martha, was not athletic. She was beautiful, funny, smart, insightful, and special in many ways. Athletic she was not. In my mind, I had always imagined sharing recreational activities with my future wife. After all, everyone can throw a Frisbee, right? Hmmm. Let's move on.

Martha and I have different ideas about money. Our families come from different political parties. She and I require different amounts of sleep. One makes long-term plans. The other is spontaneous. She carries some classic characteristic traits of being the middle child. I am the baby of my family. Martha is more than an able dancer. Her Latin blood kicks in on the dance floor and she moves with grace and ease. I have a flair for awkwardness when dancing and avoid the activity at all costs. Her mother spent years in an orphanage and came to the States unable to speak English. My grandmother was one of the first women to graduate with a master's degree from her prestigious alma mater.

I could go on and on and list more unique things about our backgrounds and differences. These are not challenges, obstacles, disappointments, or complications. Our differences, family histories, preferences, and predispositions contribute to, not hinder, what was created when we became a couple. However, I did not always have this view. Some of our differences I viewed as challenges and regrets early in our marriage. This constricted view only increased the likelihood of unhappiness and discontentment—the very things I wanted to avoid.

There is a better reality to embrace. Martha does not have to be athletic for me to cherish her. I don't have to bust a move to be the love of her life. When our hearts and lives were joined we became something unique and special. There is no other creation like us. We love and celebrate what we have become as a couple. Incidentally, we have found recreational activities to enjoy together, but they don't involve a ball, club, or racket. We enjoy dancing, but it doesn't require loud music or a public venue (for which the patrons should be grateful!).

PATIO
19'0" x 8'0"
BREAKFAST ROOM
12'6" x 11'9"
LIVING ROOM
19'11" x 20'6"
MASTER BEDROOM
12'2" x 16'0"
STORAGE
UTILITY
CLOSET
KITCHEN
12'7" x 13'3"
CLOSET
GARAGE
19'9" x 19'8"
MASTER BATH
PANTRY
POWDER ROOM
HALL
BATH #2
FOYER
6'8" x 17'8"
CLOSET
CLOSET
FORMAL ROOM
11'6" x 13'5"
NURSERY
11'9" x 12'
PORCH
OFFICE
10'6" x 12'3"

THREE

The Blueprint

Every construction work has a plan. It's called a blueprint. The blueprint provides *guidance*. Before building, review the blueprint guidelines. The blueprint will help you build successfully.

You have the right tools:

- Practicing Empathetic Listening
- Choosing Dialogue over Discussion; which fosters Transparency and Open-mindedness
- Embracing the Uniqueness and Beauty of your Relationship.

Now follow the blueprint:

Beginning in the next chapter, you will start to walk through your house. As mentioned, in each room you will find a series of case studies. Each case study is based on a true incident or situation, though I have changed the names and taken some editorial license for clarity. The couples in the case studies experienced significant hardship. You are to give honest thought and reflection on how to counsel the couple in each study. Share what advice and guidance you would give to the couple with your partner. Explore possibilities and various scenarios. Listen empathetically to your partner as they share their advice and suggestions. You will discover your spouse's feelings and thoughts regarding significant issues. Remember, the goal is to have meaningful communication with your mate, not necessarily agree on how the problems in the case study should be addressed. Situations in each case provide avenues that allow you to explore the heart of your mate. After each case study you will see a set of questions. The questions are more direct. They are written to help facilitate a time of transparency and discovery.

Blueprint: Four Guidelines for Building

1. Discovery

One of the beautiful things couples experience during courtship is discovery. You discover *the way* he likes his coffee. You discover *the way* her hair falls to one side of her face when she raises her head. You realize *the way* he is drawn to tinker with gadgets. You become aware of *the way* she connects with first-time acquaintances. Discovery is a significant part of courtship. We are attracted to each other's *way*.

After years of being together, couples often become too busy to enjoy discovery. We fail to appreciate the very things that drew us together in the first place. Occasionally, over time, his or her way actually annoys us! Reviewing the case studies and exploring the questions will prompt discovery. You have an opportunity to discover each other's way. Some questions will lead you to discuss worldviews, beliefs, and ethics. Life philosophies and moral standards will be exposed. A person's moral standard and value system greatly influences perspective and behavior. You will learn something you did not know. Enjoy discovery all over again.

2. Schedule "Room Nights"

Usually, if things are going to get done, they need to be scheduled. Couples who take a six-week premarital class reserve those dates on the calendar and attend the classes. Families that enroll their children in a sports activity secure the team's game schedule and protect those dates from other conflicts. It is highly recommended that you schedule "room nights." Go to a cozy coffee shop or make plans to have breakfast on the back porch on a Saturday morning; unplug the TV, close the laptop, and do whatever else is necessary to spend time with your beloved. They deserve it. You deserve it. If meaningful communication with your partner nurtures happiness and intimacy, isn't it worth the time?

3. Decorate

These are your rooms. Decorate as you see fit. Like any decoration, the beauty is in the eye of the beholder. Change the paint color, select your taste in wall art, and add a few throw pillows. What I mean is, focus on each other and what brings depth and life to the conversation. Just continue to use the right tools and follow the blueprint.

So, if there is a case study or question that does not help facilitate meaningful communication, skip it. If the children's room of your home is firing on all cylinders, there is little need to speed a lot of time there. It is unlikely that each room needs the same attention. Spend your valuable time in a room, case study, or particular question that stretches your need for empathetic listening, transparency, openness, and dialogue. This is where you will benefit as you pursue meaningful conversation. Going through all the rooms and answering every question is not the point. Increasing vitality in your relationship with meaningful conversation is the point. If that is accomplished by spending time in only one room, mission accomplished. Additionally, if there is a question or case study that is close to a personal wound or current struggle, skip this area if empathetic listening and dialogue cannot be achieved.

Another decorating necessity is the phrase, "I'm sorry." Either out of pride or insecurity, some people would rather die a thousand deaths than to voice a sincere apology; however, an honest expression of regret and sorrow is beautiful and attractive. Like empathetic listening, apologies fuel connection:

> "I flew off the handle and said things that hurt you. I'm very sorry for my anger and the wounds it caused."

> "I belittled your personal story and that was rude of me. I was wrong and insensitive. I am very sorry."

An apology is not a sign of weakness. We usually do not think less of one who apologizes. We typically hold them in higher esteem. An apology is a beautiful expression of hope and recovery. It brings color and life to the relationship. Sometimes we think only *big* offenses merit an apology, but small bricks can build high walls of separation. Apologies are great brick removers.

4. Curb Appeal

Before we enter your home, briefly consider "curb appeal," i.e., mutual attraction. We are going to accept the fact that you are mutually attracted to each other! What caused this initial attraction? Was it the eyes, the swagger, the crinkle of the nose during laughter, a passion for justice, interest in art history, love for the theater, religious faith, the six-pack, or tight blue jeans? You partner wants to hear. What caused this wonderful curb appeal?

An actual home has curb appeal to certain people. They like the wrap-around porch. They like the big oak tree. They like the bay window. For whatever reason, these things appeal to the buyer.

Tell your partner what you find appealing about him or her. I love being told I am a good dad. I love being told I am a good listener. I love being appreciated for planning a great vacation. Even if I am not the best parent, listener, or vacation planner, I'm still blessed when my wife tells me these qualities appeal to her.

As I was writing this book, Martha yelled across the room one evening, "I'm washing the shirts of my love." Her statement was an affirming word clothed in service and commitment. Later that week I said to her, "You are my favorite person." To be someone's favorite is appealing, right? Sappy? It could be, but who cares? The truth is we probably don't voice these sentiments to each other enough. It would be misleading to have you think Martha and I have these kinds of exchanges daily, but I do want her to regularly know she appeals to me, and I want to hear it from her. Every heart craves affirmation, attention, and affection. We shouldn't be shy or hesitant about giving it in a manner that is natural and beneficial. Such comments bless the giver and the recipient. Please interject curb appeal moments before, during, and after your room conversations.

Okay, all you Bobs and Carolines (which we all are to some degree), let's take a look at your home. We are going to walk through your home room by room. Each room represents an area of life. Talk about things that matter to you in each room. Together you will discover each other's values and perspectives in fresh ways. You will disclose thoughts on how you want to live. Reflect on how you can express love in a way that supports the life your mate wants to live.

Moving is essential

I had one person read the unpublished manuscript and say, "Is your book intended to discourage marriage? All your case studies are about couples engaged in disagreement and angst."

The book is not intended to discourage marriage at all. Marriage is an amazing creation filled with wonder and wooing that takes people to places of bliss and beauty like no other. And healthy marriages are so deeply needed. The health and happiness of the home plays a significant role in the health and happiness of society—on so many levels. But let's be honest, many marriages experience hardship and struggle. This book is designed to help couples face challenges and common causes of discord in a constructive way. I said *constructive* way. Remember, we are builders. We build *constructively*.

When engineers and construction workers design and erect skyscrapers, they design and build the structure to endure storms. Storms come in all shapes, sizes, strengths, and durations. If the structure is not properly prepared for these winds of force, the building suffers. Skyscrapers are purposely designed to sway in heavy winds. They are designed to move. Because of their movement they endure storms and remain standing after the winds have calmed. And so it is with marriage and any other relationship. The forces of nature, circumstance, selfishness, weariness, and plain old mood swings generate relational gale winds that bring pressure to all relationships. We need to be designed, constructed, and prepared to move. Moving is essential!

FOUR

Formal Room

Maybe your house does not have a "formal" room. (And if it does, and you have preschoolers, it may have become a game room!) But the formal room of your home has great significance in maintaining a healthy and happy relationship.

I'm sure some of you know that in the 1950s and 60s the furniture in some formal rooms was covered in plastic. The reason was to protect the furniture. In some ways, that is how our conversations are with our spouses in public or "formal" places. In those places, we are more inclined to guard our conversations. We protect ourselves. The way we talk in public is often different than how we communicate behind closed doors. The formal room asks the question, *"How shall we live in public?"* How shall we act around other people, and does that pattern of behavior foster happiness and intimacy?

A little kidding and poking fun at each other can energize a relationship. These jabs need to be at appropriate levels and remain fun and funny. Otherwise, we take pokes on the chin. When we are struck in unkind ways it weakens the relational bond. Are we aware of those lines? Are our little jabs more of a jolt than we think, leaving bruises beneath the surface? We are going to focus on three areas of public behavior: how we talk, how we act, and how we interact.

CASE STUDY I

Kim has had enough. She feels like a punching bag. Her husband, Ryan, made another comment about her inability to cook. They were out on the town dining with two other couples. When Ryan was glancing at the menu he noticed the pot roast and offered to the table, "Pot roast sounds good. The last time Kim attempted to cook it, I ate the roast and spent most of my night on the pot!" He continued, "When we call the kids to the dinner table, they don't ask what we are having, they ask if mom cooked. If I tell them yes, they groan as if I told them they were grounded for a week." Ryan then backpedaled. He placed his hand on Kim's shoulder and said, "Oh honey, you know I'm playing. It's not that bad." Kim confronts Ryan at home about his comments and he shrugs it off saying he was just playing. But Ryan's behavior doesn't change. He really does not think he is doing anything wrong. It's all in fun. Kim does not want to have social outings with Ryan anymore because of his ongoing mockery. Ryan is upset about her decision. Kim suggests they visit a therapist to address the matter. Ryan is unwilling and thinks this whole thing is blown way out of proportion. What would your advice be for this couple?

Questions:

- What do you think about Ryan's sense of humor? Does it help to know that when others tease him in that way, he thinks it's funny? This really is his favorite form of humor.

- What kind of lines should a person draw in public so feelings are not hurt and no one is cast in a bad light?
- Is there a place or time of day that is best for serious conversation?
- What are you most sensitive about when it comes to your person? Can you be oversensitive?
- Some people view being rude or plainspoken as simply being authentic. What kind of authenticity is acceptable for the general public? Your friends? Your family?
- What kinds of conversations are reserved only for your spouse?

CASE STUDY 2

Ruth is tired of being treated like one of the boys. Greg romanced her well when they were dating. In the early years of marriage he continued to cater to her needs. He opened car doors for her. He opened doors to all building entrances for her. He would not let her carry groceries from the car to the kitchen or put the trash out by the curb. He knew when her car needed fuel and filled the gas tank so she would not have to. Over the years this kind of care and attention has gradually stopped. When Ruth mentions to Greg how he used to care for her, he rolls his eyes and says, "I can't do everything, honey." Ruth is sad with the state of her marriage and would like to revitalize their relationship. She voices this to Greg periodically, but he continues to scoff at her suggestion. What advice do you have for Greg and Ruth?

Questions:

- Do you think "getting too comfortable" in marriage is unavoidable? Is that something that will occur over the natural course of time? Why or why not?
- Are there things that occur during the courtship stage that should not continue during marriage?
- When appreciation and care erodes in a relationship, what might be done to address this concern?

- When does expressing concern over a matter become nagging?
- Would it be best for the relationship if Ruth would just stop expressing concern and the need for "revitalizing" their relationship?
- What other issues below the surface might be stirring in this story?

CASE STUDY 3

"Breathe. Stop talking and take a breath," Mark thinks as he observes his wife's constant talking at the dinner table. He always knew Lana was engaging and outgoing. She could strike up chitchat with anyone. He always admired that quality about her; however, after five years of marriage, her range for controlling the conversation has increased five-fold. If table conversation were a Monopoly board, she would have a hotel on every property. Mark enjoys hearing the opinions of others around the dinner table, but Lana regulates the flow and permits only a certain number of words per person before she takes over.

Maybe Mark is overreacting. Everyone at the dinner table seems to really enjoy her storytelling. But when Mark tries to contribute to the conversation he feels Lana's insistent babbling always cuts him off. He feels she doesn't even notice he's trying to participate. Lana's control is primarily in the company of others, but it spills over into other areas of the home. Mark feels like a child, instructed in what he can and can't do.

He tries to bring the issue to her attention, but it is quickly dismissed. He feels disconnected to Lana. Mark recently filled out a profile on an internet dating site. He would like to have dinner with someone who would listen to him. What advice do you have for this couple?

Questions:

- Do you have a trait or characteristic that can come across as negative in some way?
- Do you see yourself as generally open to "suggestions" from your partner regarding social behaviors? Why or why not?
- Do you think Mark is overreacting? Do you think Lana is underreacting?
- What situations in marriage require forms of intervention?
- What other information or factors in this story would be important to know in giving advice to this couple?

CASE STUDY 4

Rachael is married to Jeremy. Jeremy got a call from his friend and coworker, Fran, who is in a dating relationship with William. Fran and William have hit a few rough spots in their dating relationship. Jeremy and William are not close friends, but they know and like each other. Fran is seeking advice on her relationship with William and called Jeremy to ask if they could discuss some of the issues. Because Jeremy and Fran work in the same building, they were able to step out that week during the lunch hour, grab a bite to eat, and discuss Fran's concerns about William. Over the next two weeks, Fran and Jeremy had lunch together twice.

One evening Jeremy mentions to his wife, Rachael, that he met with Fran twice to discuss her relationship quandaries. Rachael has met Fran. Fran is fairly attractive and Rachael is uncomfortable with her husband meeting with her, and she asks him not to do it again. Jeremy is taken aback by Rachael's stance and believes her expression is rooted in a lack of trust. This is very disconcerting to him. He honestly has no interest in Fran whatsoever. Jeremy, now wounded, does not want to be controlled by Rachael in this way. There is an ongoing standoff on this topic. What would your counsel to this couple be?

Questions:

- Is it ever appropriate or acceptable to have a "friendly" relationship with the opposite sex? Why or why not?
- How do you define "friendly," and what boundaries should be set for interacting with the opposite sex?
- If you are at a wedding or another social event and see a man dance with another man's wife, do any concerns surface in your mind?
- How do you prefer to interact in public settings such as company events, social functions, or a block party? For example, is there value in mingling independently, or do you want to mingle as a couple?
- There are many concerns related to this case study. Some couples share Facebook and email accounts to help protect the marriage. What are some good practices that might provide reasonable protection to most marriages?
- What are some challenges inherent to this story and other cultural norms?

On a personal note

In the aforementioned case study, I happen to know that Rachael and Jeremy's standoff included a variety of ugly verbal exchanges over several weeks. Ugly verbal exchanges drain relational equity. Some of the best advice my wife and I received prior to getting married was on the matter of talking to each other. Our premarital counselor said to us, "Now when you fight (and you will), fight right." He went on to suggest a few ground rules for fighting. He suggested that sarcasm be off-limits. Sarcasm, by its nature, minimizes the feelings of another person. When directed at someone, sarcasm provokes and belittles. Martha and I were very capable of using sarcasm as a weapon to defend and cut. We both decided to bury that hatchet early in our marriage.

The counselor also told us that bringing up past offenses was to be off-limits. I was guilty of this. Instead of staying on one issue during an argument, there was the temptation to bring up past offenses to build and make my case. Bringing up past offenses is an action intended to harm. It is never a tool used to resolve, but to offend. I could bring up a list of offenses with great ease. These offenses didn't even have to be accurately recalled. I was just reaching for ammunition during the argument. Bringing up past offenses was another weapon of war we buried, alongside the hatchet of sarcasm. Doing so has served us well.

How we talk to each other matters.

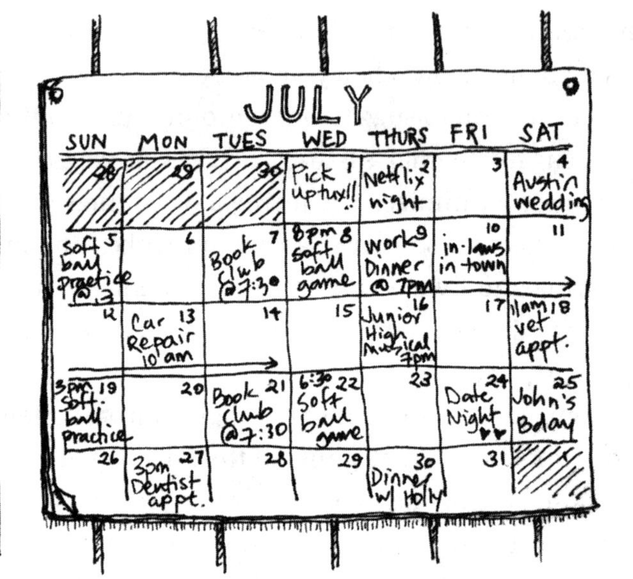
JULY
SUN MON TUES WED THURS FRI SAT
Pick up tux!!
Netflix night
Austin wedding
Soft ball practice @3
Book club @7:30
8pm soft ball game
work Dinner @ 7pm
in-laws in town
Car Repair 10 am
Junior High Musical 7pm
11am vet appt.
3pm soft ball practice
Book club @7:30
6:30 soft ball game
Date Night
John's Bday
3pm Dentist appt.
Dinner w/ Holly

FIVE

Living Room

The living room is where we spend most of our time as a couple and family. The living room asks the question, *"How shall we live* together?" There are hundreds of areas to explore. Explore them! If you get to a subject mentioned, like Traditions or Education, and that case study opens up six other "case studies" that come to mind, delve into those situations and circumstances. Remember to use the right "tools" as you build healthy conversations.

CASE STUDY I - EDUCATION

Ian loves to learn. He went back to school and earned his real estate license last year. The year before he studied a semester of photography. Currently he is taking a course to become a certified scuba instructor, and he is also giving thought to learning another language at the local junior college. Hope, his wife, is concerned that too much time and money are being spent on things that are not beneficial to the family. What are some potential root issues you see for Ian and Hope? How might agreement and support be reached?

Questions:

- Do you consider yourself a natural learner?
- Do you have challenges when it comes to certain kinds of learning styles? Do you prefer auditory or visual training?
- Do you follow instructions or would you rather experiment?
- Do you respect people more who have a college degree than those who do not?
- Do you desire to continue formal or informal education in some way?

- For your children, what are your hopes for their education? What roles will you play in their educational journey?
- What other questions about education come to mind when you consider how you would like to live?

CASE STUDY 2 - ALCOHOL

Joseph and Karen have been married ten years. In recent months Karen decides to have a glass of wine at the end of most days. One glass often turns into two. Joseph is not fundamentally opposed to alcohol, but he is concerned. He believes the wine negatively affects Karen. She sees no difference in her behavior. The issue has caused a deep divide in the marriage. What should be the course of action for each of them? What advice would you offer?

Questions:

- Karen could see no difference in her behavior. We are all somewhat blinded, at times, about our behavior. How open are you to having your partner evaluate your behavioral tendencies?
- Regarding your eating and drinking habits, is your spouse welcome to speak a word of caution to you regarding your dietary practices or alcohol consumption?
- How might alcohol negatively affect children? In what ways and at what age should children be exposed to alcohol?
- What other nuances of this topic should be considered?

CASE STUDY 3 - VOCATION

Dustin got into the hospitality industry because the buzz of an active restaurant fuels him. The customers know him by name, and the owner is happy with the way he manages the place. However, his work schedule is consuming. This schedule was acceptable during the years the couple did not have children. Janie, his wife, was willing to adjust and endure. She accepted the fact that he would be absent most evenings. But now that the kids are old enough to participate in evening school activities, Janie would like for Dustin to support them and be present at their performances. Dustin has made some concessions to be available at certain family events viewed as "important," but he is still absent most evenings. Janie is friends with the owner of the restaurant and called to see if her husband could focus on the lunch crowd and allow her husband to be free eighty percent of the evenings. The owner agreed. Did she do the right thing? What could have been done differently? How many scenarios, both positive and negative, might be played out here?

Questions:

- If you have a vocational dream, share that with your partner. How can you help your spouse fulfill that dream?

- What are the key factors that lead you to a certain vocation? Salary? Aptitude? Personal fulfillment? Flexibility of schedule? Particular benefits?
- What factors should be considered when evaluating the importance of a job when it relates to family decisions (like relocating, or taking leave if home childcare is needed)?
- If one of you put a lot of time, money, and education toward mastering a certain vocation and then decided to pursue something totally different, would that be okay? What if the new vocational pursuit was less lucrative?

CASE STUDY 4 - HOBBIES/RECREATION/ENTERTAINMENT

Ricky and Val have been married for almost eighteen months. Her frustration has grown to the point of wanting to end the marriage. When Ricky was single and in his early twenties, he spent a lot of time gaming on the computer. Now that they are living under the same roof and he is about to turn thirty, his gaming activity has not slowed down. He spends almost twenty hours a week gaming and stays up late at night. He scoffs at Val's objections and says; "You knew I was an avid gamer and night owl before we married. Why are you on my case about this?" What should each of them do? What advice might you offer Ricky and Val?

Questions:

- What expectations or modifications should Ricky and Val consider?
- Might there be a deeper issue than gaming and late nights?
- What are your favorite games and why?
- Are you a good loser? Are you a good winner?
- How would you describe your competitive side?
- How much and what kind of television viewing is acceptable in the home?

- Is there a hobby you hope to take up in the future?
- Is there anything you hope to start doing together for fun?

CASE STUDY 5 - TIME

Grant believes in making the most of his time. Every Saturday morning he starts his day with a morning run, reads a little, and hopes to have several "to-dos" accomplished before noon. Sylvia loves to sleep in on Saturdays until 9:00 a.m. At 10:00 a.m. she is on her second cup of coffee, in her PJs, and still "waking up." To him, she is lazy and wasting valuable time. To her, he is hyper and—on Saturdays—a pest. How would you counsel these two?

Questions:

- What would be your leaning on a day off, Grant or Sylvia's style?
- What do you like to do with your discretionary time?
- Are you a procrastinator?
- How much time should couples spend apart from each other?
- In what ways do you value rest and recreation?
- In what ways do you value time spent accomplishing something?
- In what ways do you feel rushed or anxious by the clock?
- Are you upset if you arrive somewhere "late"? What is "late" to you?

- If opposites attract, is it okay to "be" opposite and just live with it?
- For Grant and Sylvia, should either be concerned about what the other does with their time? Why or why not?

CASE STUDY 6 - FRIENDS

Dawn comes out and says it. "It's not that I don't like people. I like people fine. I'm with people at work and they like me and I like them. I just don't *need* people. I don't need a girls' night out. I don't need to have another couple to hang out with. Why do you want an abundance of friends, and why do you spend every weekend with a buddy or two? I thought you married me to spend time with me. Can't we just be together?" She is exasperated. Her husband, Len, is taken aback. He was just trying to be helpful. He sees Dawn more and more withdrawn and wants to encourage her social life. He values friendships a great deal. What counsel would you offer them?

Questions:

- What might be some underlying issues with this couple?
- What traits do you value most in friendships?
- Do some people need more friends than others? If so, why might that be?
- What is your hope and desire in the friendships you have?
- How can friendships develop into unhealthy relationships?

- What is the balance of friendship you would like to see in your life? As a couple?
- What characteristics do you possess that make you a good friend?
- What traits or behavioral patterns might challenge your ability to make, maintain, or keep friends?
- What other considerations around this topic should be voiced when you reflect on how you would like to live?

CASE STUDY 7 - FAITH

After five years of marriage, Amber was weary. She and her husband, Keith, had both discussed the value of faith, and both agreed they were going to be people who lived out their faith; however, his vigor for religious living grew at a much faster rate than hers. Keith is more avid about church attendance, service to the church, and mission activities than what Amber prefers. She started to resent him, and she eventually began resenting God. She thinks Keith has gone overboard, but then she thinks, "How can I compete with God?!" She regularly feels like she is a "bad" person and that she is unable to live in a way that pleases Keith. Keith wants to encourage her participation, but does not want to be pushy. He tries to be sensitive to the difference. How might this couple reach a healthy and happy place regarding their faith? How would you encourage each of them?

Questions:

- What if a husband and wife were not very religious at the start of their relationship, but one of them experienced a dramatic change and felt the need to serve God in a significant way?
- In what ways can Amber support Keith without feeling like she is drowning? How should Keith be sensitive to Amber? What are the best ways for them to share the matter of faith in a mutually respectful way?

- Do you hope to grow in your faith?
- Do you expect faith to be shared with your spouse and agreed upon in doctrine and practice?
- If you belong to a church, what is your philosophy and purpose for being a church member? How do you define "involvement and commitment" as it relates to church?
- Should couples that share the same faith pray together? What might that look like?

CASE STUDY 8 - IN-LAWS

Terri is adamant, "They just want to help!" Her husband, Jimmy, responds back to his bride, "No, they want to control." It is a nice couch. It is an expensive couch. Terri is not a big fan of the couch, but it works for her. Jimmy hates the couch, but maybe he only "hates" the couch because of where it came from. Terri's parents purchased the new couch to "help" them decorate and get settled in their small apartment. Terri and Jimmy want and need a couch, but money is tight and they cannot afford to purchase anything half as nice. A gift of matching furniture could very well follow this generous gesture from Terri's parents. Jimmy believes the couch ought to be sent back. Terri feels that if they decline the couch or exchange it, her mother's feelings would be hurt and her parents might withhold their generosity. What do you think Terri and Jimmy should do in this situation?

Questions:

- Many parents enjoy helping their children. Is Jimmy overreacting? Is Terri underreacting or selling out?

- Traditionally, when couples marry they "leave" their parents and "cleave" to their new mate. How do you interpret leaving and cleaving?

- If your spouse's relationship with your parents is challenging (or even borders on hostile), what can you do to help manage and reduce the tension?
- What kind of involvement from in-laws should be expected during holidays or regular patterns of life?
- With regard to personal concerns (like how one raises a child), what guidelines or boundaries should be agreed upon?
- What can you tell your spouse about your family dynamics (include siblings and other significant family members) that will help him or her interact and understand your family better?
- What are your biggest fears about connecting with your in-laws?
- What is the best way for you to encourage your in-laws?

CASE STUDY 9 - PETS

Sajan questioned why his beloved parrots expired sooner than the normal life expectancy of most parrots. Maybe it had something to do with the fact that every time his wife, Joanna, passed the caged bird with an aerosol can of furniture polish, hair spray, or insect repellent, she would spray the parrot in the face. Sajan was never around to witness this action. (Believe it or not, this case study, like all the others in this book, is based on a true event.) What is the root problem in this situation? What are some conversations that need to happen between this husband and wife?

Questions:

- Usually the problem with a pet is not the pet. It is everything that comes with the animal. What things about owning a pet please you? What things displease you?
- If a pet is important to your spouse, to what degree should the pet be important to you?
- What other "pet-like" issues might be worth mentioning?

CASE STUDY 10 - HYGIENE

Courtney's idea of "dirty" is different than Carl's. She is self-diagnosed OCD and he is admittedly grimy. She bathes twice a day at minimum. He likes his "natural" smell. Before marriage, she simply chose to overlook a lot of things that would normally have bothered her, and during courtship, Carl had put his best foot forward toward cleanliness. He made every attempt to tidy up and be as presentable as possible. The marriage is less than a year old, and the matter of hygiene has become a painful thorn in each one's side. What advice would you give them?

Questions:

- If you have bad breath or body odor, or were wearing dirty clothes, would you want your partner to mention it to you?

How adaptable or conscientious would you be to please your spouse's expectations of cleanliness? How do you feel about the following true-life examples?

- One husband asked his wife to step into the shower area to apply hair spray. This way, he pointed out, the bathroom floor does not become sticky. This might not be a big request at all in your home—but then again, it might be.

- One wife asked her husband to never leave anything in the sink. The dishwasher was the appropriate place for all dirty utensils, bowls, plates, and cups. She would really appreciate it if *nothing* were ever left in the sink. This might not be a big request at your home—but then again, it might be.

Do you know of any practice or preference that might be considered an abnormal peeve that you insist your family follow because it is *that* important to you? How do you feel about these true-life examples?

- One mom became annoyed if anyone in the family used a paper towel in place of a dinner napkin.
- One dad would not allow his kids to use steak sauce on steaks he cooked at the house. He believed it ruined the taste of a great steak.
- People from some cultures do not wear shoes inside the home. Instead, shoes are removed upon entrance into the home.
- What other matters of this nature are worth exploring?

CASE STUDY II - TRADITIONS

Marina's family's tradition is to do Christmas *big*. "Big" means lots of presents, lots of interior decorations, and lots of outside lights. Presents are never to be need-based, practical items. Don's heritage, on the other hand, is extremely practical in every area of life, including gift giving. Gifts, while not cheap or thoughtless, are to be practical and given in moderation. As a couple, this discovery about each other's practice is disturbing for both Don and Marina. Doing Christmas *big* requires a lot of planning, expense, time, and energy many weeks before Christmas Day. Her attitude about Christmas is the same for other holidays and birthdays. So, several times a year Don withdraws and mopes because of Marina's *big* interest in holidays and special occasions. Several times a year she cries because of his lack of support and concern. Holidays and birthdays are challenging experiences in this home. What would be your counsel to Don and Marina?

Questions:

- What were your favorite holiday or special occasion traditions as a child?
- Which tradition do you hope to continue or start as a couple?
- What other things in life do you like to do over-the-top more than others?

- What things in life do you generally play down more than others?
- What was your favorite gift to receive as a child and why?
- Do you remember the earliest time you thoughtfully gave a gift to someone else? What was the gift and why was that experience special to you?

CASE STUDY 12 - MEDICAL

"Didn't you just go to the doctor last week?" Derek asked. It isn't that he does not care about Jessica's health. It's not that he is fundamentally opposed to doctors. He just believes that going to a doctor is the result of an emergency. He feels that if a person has a bruise, cold, or an ache, that person will get better over time and there is no need to visit a doctor. Jessica values a doctor's opinion and seeks professional medical advice when she has a medical concern. She also has legitimate hormone and headache issues for which she takes prescribed medications. When he questions her trips to the doctor, she feels disrespected and treated like a child. He wonders if the frequency of her trips is "normal" and if the financial costs are wasteful. How would you counsel this couple?

Questions:

- When you are sick, do you like to be waited on, or left alone?
- Do you typically have an annual physical?
- How important and how often do you have your teeth cleaned by a dentist?
- What home remedies or nontraditional methods of care do you practice and hope to see your family practice?

- Are you inclined to use prescription drugs? What are your opinions on alternative medicines and treatments?
- If a person you love were overmedicating, how would you go about helping them?
- Are there any medical conditions in your family?
- If you had to categorize any phobias you might have related to health, medicines, or doctors, what would they be?
- Do you fear death, disease, or severe health limitations?

CASE STUDY 13 - EMPTY NEST AND AUTUMN YEARS

Clare and Tanner have enjoyed a happy marriage together. Clare lost her first husband to cancer after nine years of marriage. She was thirty-three years old when her husband died. She met Tanner on a blind date two years later. He was recovering from a nasty divorce. Clare and Tanner will celebrate twenty years of marriage next June. They are in their early sixties.

Tanner's oldest son, Thomas, is thirty-four. Thomas has had a string of issues. He is twice divorced, and most everyone believes his irresponsible behavior led to the end of those marriages. He is a substance abuser and has difficulty keeping a job. Thomas is currently in need of a place to stay so he can get back on his feet and find employment. Tanner is softhearted and loves his son. He tells Thomas he can move in with him and Clare.

In Clare's mind, all kinds of red flags appear. It's not that she doesn't want to help. She does. Her concern is that Thomas will upset the system and rhythm of the home if there are not clear guidelines and a plan. She does not want a permanent addition to the home. Clare's mother is eighty-six and needs to transition out of her living situation since she requires regular assistance. Clare is thinking that her mom could live with them for a year or so. Clare is also thinking about travel plans for Tanner and herself during early retirement.

Tanner suggests that Clare's mom be placed in a retirement home so she can be with people her own age. He thinks those relationships are healthy and important. Clare is insulted at the suggestion. Tanner also said to hold off on any extended travel plans. He still enjoys working and has a few irons in the fire that might not allow him to travel or retire anytime soon. It has been twenty good years of marriage, but the current issues at hand are creating arguments and extreme frustration. What might you suggest to this couple?

Questions:

- What should be considered when making a decision to have aging parents or a needy adult child move in with you?
- What do you look forward to the most when you think about your autumn years?
- What is your idea of retirement and when do you hope to retire?
- How important is it to live near or regularly see your children and grandchildren?
- What is your view of assisted living facilities for your parents? What about for your spouse or yourself?
- What do you fear most about aging?

SIX

Kitchen and Laundry Room

Questions that originate from the kitchen and laundry room are frequent. *What's for supper? Who can pick up the cleaning? Oh, wait. I forgot to take the clothes to the cleaners!* Long before dishwashers were installed in homes, a couple would stand at the kitchen sink and one would say, "I'll wash, you dry." Domestic needs are ongoing and never ending. The distribution of domestic chores can always be a moving target. These rooms ask the question, *"How shall we manage domestic responsibilities and duties?"*

For some, the division and sharing of family responsibilities is very easy. One woman told me, "Anything that requires a tool or needs to be repaired, any matter that takes place in the garage, or any need that occurs outside is his responsibility. Anything inside the house is my responsibility." For this couple, that arrangement worked. They never discussed who washed and folded clothes, who cooked, who scrubbed toilets, who repaired the leaky faucet, who mulched the flower beds, or who cleaned out the gutters. Good for them.

Over the last few decades lines and boundaries for traditional gender-specific duties have changed. Lines are not so clear or determined. There are women who tinker with broken appliances, and there are men who regularly see to the cooking or laundry needs. The purpose of walking through the kitchen and laundry room is not to determine household duties. It is to provide clarity on each other's perspective and preference. Listen empathetically, and pursue discovery and understanding.

CASE STUDY I

Alice and Adam want a maid service. However, they have run the numbers, and it is just not in the household budget. Alice and Adam both love the outdoors. Both love to get their hands dirty caring for the yard. Both do good work cutting and trimming the lawn and bushes. But both hate to dust, mop, vacuum, or do any inside chores. Cleaning a toilet is the last thing either wants to do, but they are neat people and both desire a clean house. Alice announces, "The obvious solution is to take turns doing the inside chores."

Adam begrudges that decision. His dad never had to clean a toilet or do other household chores. He tries to trade and barter other duties with Alice in order to not clean the bathrooms. She refuses and sternly responds, "We. Take. Turns." There would be no negotiation. However, over time, Adam always forgot his turn. When push came to shove and he *did* take his turn, the cleaning was inadequate. Alice would perform a quick clean of the bathroom as needed, but she hated cleaning when it wasn't her turn. While she was cleaning, she would curse Adam under her breath. This was an ongoing source of conflict and tension in the home. The anger it produced started to affect other areas of their marriage to the point that both Adam and Alice began to shut down. What words of guidance would you offer this couple?

Questions:

- Would it be fair to tend only to the domestic responsibilities that you care about?
- Is "taking turns" the best option in a situation like this?
- Could Adam's attempt at picking up additional duties be a reasonable course to suggest? Why or why not?
- What other underlying concerns do you see?

CASE STUDY 2

Shirley was often trying new things. There was always a new remedy, a short cut, or a better way. About three years ago Shirley started to dive into "healthy" eating. Organic was the new fad. Everything had to be organic. Gluten-free became another catchphrase in the home. "She's on a new kick," Lewis believed, "It will pass."

But it didn't pass. Shirley started to read labels. All the fine print of every product purchased was carefully reviewed and researched. Lewis didn't know if he was ever going to have the pleasure of eating a candy bar in her presence again without feeling guilty.

"Okay!" Lewis shouted one day, "Enough is enough. We have been on this health-kick thing for more than a year now. I'm hun-grrr-ee! I'm in favor of watching what we eat. I'm in favor of eating healthy portions to ensure we do not overeat. Yes, I agree obesity is a problem in our country, but I think our household food limitations are way overboard and out of whack. I insist we put some food choices back on the acceptable list."

Shirley can't believe what she is hearing. She's never felt physically better! She wants the best for her family and believes how she feeds her children is extremely important. She has worked hard to implement this healthful-eating lifestyle. To alter the course now is nonnegotiable for her. Positions on the issue are firm and neither is backing down. What suggestions and insights do you have for this couple?

Questions:

- How would you describe the importance of health and fitness to you and your family?
- What health and fitness standards should be encouraged and what practices should be required?
- With increased interest in freshly prepared foods, there will be more trips to the store and more time required for preparing meals. Is this the best use of time or will other areas of life suffer?
- How important is it to eat together as a family? Why or why not?
- How important is it to eat out? How often do you hope to eat out and at what kinds of restaurants?
- If you value eating out, why is that? Is it because you dislike cooking, because it is convenient, or because you don't like cleaning up a messy kitchen?
- What kinds of foods do you like to keep in the house? Do you have any special diets you would like to follow? Is it important that sweets are kept on hand?
- Many would agree that American families have become negligent in the area of health and fitness. In

what other areas of life have families become lax and negligent? What do you hope to do to address these matters with your family?

CASE STUDY 3

The text message said, "Cleaners, meds, and creamer." Elise knew what this meant. Ethan's clothes needed to be picked up, his medications were ready at the pharmacist, and he was upset before he left for work because he didn't have creamer for his morning coffee. His text was a reminder for Elise to run these errands at the end of her workday. What went through her mind was the inconvenience. Elise hated to run errands. After all, it was not her shirts or her prescriptions that needed to be picked up. And she drank her coffee black! Ethan worked downtown, about a fifty-minute drive from the house (the drive could be more than an hour with heavy traffic). Elise taught school in the neighborhood where they lived. If she ran the errands, both she and Ethan would arrive home about the same time. Ethan is not demanding with his requests, but sincerely believes it would be a good use of time for Elise. This allows them to be home at the same time and have the evening together. Is her frustration valid? Are his requests unreasonable? What advice would you provide this couple?

Questions:

- Is Ethan expecting too much or trying to avoid caring for his own needs?
- What kinds of things should be sacrificed for the sake of spending time together?

- How much time together and time apart is healthy for a couple?
- If you had to choose quality time over quantity of time together, what would you choose and why?
- What other thoughts around this topic should be voiced as you consider how you would like to live?

CASE STUDY 4

Wilson is just one of those guys who is on top of it. Susie is sweet, kind, and smart, but she lacks focus. Because of this, Wilson has taken it upon himself to care for most of the administrative needs of the family. He handles home and appliance repairs. He reviews health, property, and other insurances. He updates credit cards, online banking needs, and keeps record of all vehicle inspections and maintenance requirements. If there is a need to schedule an appointment with the vet, pay neighborhood association dues, replace air filters, or follow up with a requested RSVP, Wilson will handle it. Susie helps neaten up around the house and will cook and clean, but nothing is ever planned. When the couple plans a meal, Wilson ensures that all food ingredients are on hand for the preparation. The couple has been married eight years and each year Wilson has been assuming more and more of the household responsibilities.

Lately, Wilson is wondering if he has been played. Surely Susie can plan a meal. Surely she can arrange for a home serviceman when a repair is needed. Susie tends and cares for three children under the age of five. She explains to Wilson that she is completely spent at the end of the day. Caring for these young lives requires all of her time, attention, and energy. Wilson is not convinced. Susie has two afternoons off a week while the kids are in preschool, but hardly anything seems to ever get done if he doesn't do it.

Wilson, out of the blue, is thinking he might want a do-over. He wants to share a life with his spouse, not serve a spouse. What helpful thoughts would you suggest for this couple?

Questions:

- Do some people handle a home with preschoolers better than others? How might this impact a marriage?
- If someone excels in a particular area, wouldn't it be natural for him or her to oversee that area of the home? What if one, like Wilson, does so well in so many areas?
- Wilson was so steady and agreeable. Do you find it strange that he would have such a drastic change of heart?
- What other concerns do you see in this story and how would you address them?

On a personal note

After thirty years of marriage and raising three children, the kitchen and laundry room have been the most fluid rooms in our house. At times, each of us has made more adjustments, has gone the extra mile, and has carried more than our fair share as seasons and situations of life required it. Martha and I took turns going to graduate school. Our children required different kinds of attention at different stages of life, which required adjustments to each of our schedules. It was vital that we made ongoing modifications in these rooms through the years. Changes in the laundry and kitchen were in "constant motion" to keep pace with the "constant motion" and demands of living.

Disclaimer: Believe me, there were a few arguments along the way. We didn't get everything right every day. Raising preschoolers is stressful. Raising teenagers is stress on steroids. Graduate school is stress on steroids—on top of sleepless nights reading textbooks and writing papers. Adjustments are made in these rooms to express love as you help each other live.

An ongoing question each person must ask himself or herself is, "Are you ready to love your spouse in the rooms in which they live, always considering the never-ending stresses and forces that accompany the journey?" As we said earlier in the book, if you want to have a closer relationship with your mate, be willing and ready to *move*.

SEVEN

Office

Some homes have an office. Some homes have a room that the architect designed as an office, but the space has become a playroom, craft room, or a room that collects a variety of "stuff." But with or without actual office space, the office symbolizes two significant areas of life. It asks the question, *"How shall we manage our money and our careers?"*

CASE STUDY I

Connie is a firm believer in giving ten percent of the household income to certain charitable organizations. Randy is resistant to do so. His opposition is likely birthed from being raised in an underprivileged environment and the fear of not having "enough." Connie is the keeper of the books, and rather than fight about how much to give, she gives as close to ten percent as she can each month. Occasionally, she gives in secret believing that what Randy doesn't know won't hurt him. A few times Randy has become aware of Connie's secret giving. This creates significant emotional wounds for him. Connie feels justified in her giving since she is the one who has been tasked to keep the books and her salary is more than Randy's. She plans to continue to give, and he plans to continue to oppose this amount of giving. What insights and suggestions do you have for this couple?

Questions:

- What feelings might be generated when managing the household finances? Control? Power? Anxiety? Pressure? Added responsibility? An unwanted chore?

- Should couples have separate bank accounts? Should there be finances set aside considered "ours" and money set aside that is "individual" money?

- Do you consider yourself generous with your money? Why or why not?
- When you give, do you give with conditions? For example, do you only give if you have "extra"? Do you only give if the recipient does what you expect them to do with the gift?
- Are "secrets" ever appropriate in the life of a couple totally committed to each other?
- Do you fear not having "enough" financially?
- Do you hope to live in such a way that will enable you to support charitable organizations and humanitarian causes? Describe what that means to you.

CASE STUDY 2

April and Kent thrive well together. After twelve years of marriage, both really look forward to the end of each workday so they can spend time together. They parent two children, ages five and seven. April and Kent mutually agreed that she would stay home with the children as one of them is a high-functioning special needs child. Living on one income requires careful budgeting, but both agree it is worth it. Kent has been offered a new position, and it would be a substantial promotion. His salary would increase forty percent. However, the new promotion would require regular overnight travel. Most trips require around three nights away, but at times it can be up to seven. Kent believes he should decline the promotion because he doesn't want to be away from April or the kids. April knows the separation will be difficult, but the salary increase would be a big help for a number of reasons. Kent and April are disappointed with each other's perspective. Each believes the other should agree with his or her view. What kind of scenarios could be played out here? What insights and suggestions do you have for April and Kent?

Questions:

- Let's assume April and Kent both have sincere motives, void of selfish ambition, and let's assume each truly wants what is best for the family. Does this make things easier or not?

- How much say should one person have in the other person's vocational choices?
- In what ways might money buy happiness? In what ways does it fall short?
- What simple things in life bring you pleasure? What costly things bring you pleasure, and how important is it for you to secure or experience them?
- How do you measure materialism? Do you have materialistic tendencies?
- What kinds of sacrifices are you prepared to make to provide for your family?
- Do you have career goals? How important is it that you reach those goals? What are you willing to do to insure you reach them?
- What other observations do you have about this situation?

EIGHT

Children's Room

Now the party starts! Nothing changes the landscape of a home like the pitter-patter of little feet. Couples have the opportunity to enjoy sleepless nights, experience the pleasure of unbearably foul diaper odors, and share the thrill of constant whining and complaining, bringing you to the point of near insanity. Teasing aside (mostly), children are beautiful, beyond special, and captivatingly adorable. Children are the legacy of our lives. They bring about the best—and worst—of family dynamics. The children's room asks the question, *"How shall we raise our children?"*

CASE STUDY I

Amelia is a fifth-grade schoolteacher. David is an artist by trade. David and Amelia have two different parenting styles. Amelia's dad was in the military, and the pace of military life shaped her thinking. David's approach to life is very "*que sera, sera.*" In most matters of life these differences don't seem to be an issue but when it comes to parenting, the differences sow sorrows. Amelia and David have twin seventh-graders and a freshman in high school. When the children arrive home after school, Amelia insists that any and all homework be completed before playtime. She does not want her children staying up late at night or misaligning priorities.

David believes that after a hard day at school the most natural and needed thing to do is unwind. He believes that there is only so much sunlight in a day and that the kids should enjoy it! All of the children, given a choice, choose to play.

David is often with the kids when they arrive home from school. Amelia has asked David repeatedly to ensure that the kids focus on their homework right after school. David is just not convicted about that choice and rarely follows through on her request. Both feel disrespected and angry. Such stark differences make for a very long school year. What advice would you give to resolve this problem?

Questions:

- Would the personalities and achievement levels of the children impact your thoughts on the situation? Why or why not?
- How does one shape the work ethic of a child?
- Do punishments, schedules, and rewards vary from child to child depending on the need of the child?
- Do you parent for fairness or for effectiveness? What are the challenges and benefits with each approach?
- How important are grades? Would you ever consider hiring a tutor?
- What is a "balanced life" for a child?
- Do you prefer to put your child through public school, private school, or homeschool? What benefits and challenges of each situation are compelling to you?
- What other thoughts come to mind after reading this case study?

CASE STUDY 2

Tim and Toni have one daughter, Tara. Tara has her dad wrapped around her finger. So when Tara tried out for high school cheerleading and didn't make the squad, Tim went to the school and talked with the principal behind closed doors. Tim is well-connected in the community, and he insinuated he would use his connections in a way that would be unfavorable for the principal. The following Monday morning, it was announced to the student body that, after further review of the scores, Tara did qualify for one of the cheerleading spots. This outrages Toni. She believes that what Tim did set a horrible example for Tara and that Tim's helicopter parenting has not prepared their daughter for real-life consequences.

Tim says to Toni, "This is real life. People can use their influence and ability to get things done, or they can let opportunities pass them by. I saw an opportunity to help Tara become a cheerleader, something she has dreamed about for several years. Why can't a father help his daughter fulfill her dreams?"

Toni asks Tara not to take the position. Toni believes this is a valuable life lesson and that it is more important than being cheerleader her senior year. Toni also asks Tim to return to the principal and apologize for his behavior. Tim refuses. Emotions run high and both husband and wife are issuing threats and ultimatums. What kinds of developments could play out here? What counsel would you give this couple? What counsel would you offer to the daughter, Tara?

Questions:

- Is it important for children to learn through failure? In what ways?
- Is it important for children to know they have the full support of their parents? In what ways?
- Should Tara follow her mom's advice and not take the cheerleading position?
- Was asking Tara not to take the cheerleading position a fair request of Toni? Why or why not?
- What kind of pressure does Tara find herself under with her mom, dad, and the school's student body?
- Children have been known to play parents against each other. How important is it for parents to be unified? Is it more important to be unified about a matter or to be "right" about a matter?
- What other concerns come to mind from this story?

CASE STUDY 3

Erica and Allan are so grateful for one another. They are a happily married blended family. Erica has two boys, ages five and seven. Allan has an eight-year-old girl. Erica and Allan met each other at a New Year's Eve party two years ago, and they hit it off right away. Their stories are very similar. Both are just shy of thirty years old. Each married their high school sweetheart shortly after graduating. Both had their first child within the first year of marriage and divorced their spouse after four years of marriage.

Allan would like to have another child, one with Erica. Erica had a tubal ligation after the birth of her second son. Allan suggests she undergo another surgery to enable her to conceive again, but Erica is not excited about that prospect. She suggests they adopt, but Allan is not excited by the counterproposal. The idea of a fourth child continues to be one of interest, but the couple makes no progress on adoption or Erica's surgery. What thoughts might you offer to Erica and Allan?

Questions:

- What other information about Allan and Erica would help you understand the situation better?
- What are your general feelings about fostering and adoption?

- Do you think your view of adoption would be different if you were adopted?
- If you belonged to a blended family, what two things would you focus on to nurture love, belonging, and unity?
- What other thoughts does this story generate?

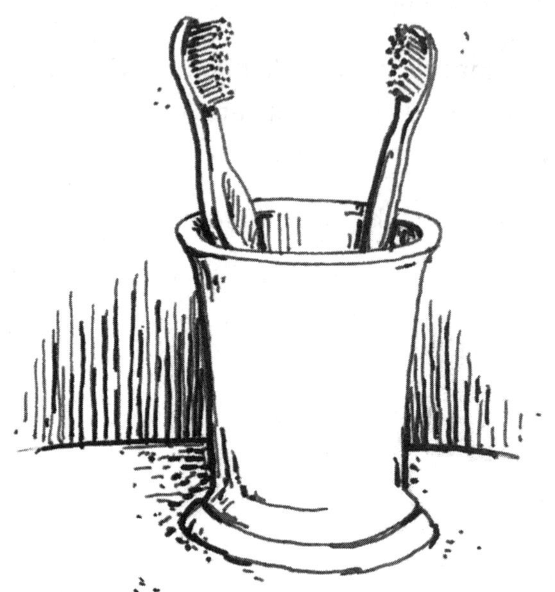

NINE
Bathroom

The bathroom is the only room that accentuates separateness. In the bathroom there are separate toothbrushes, deodorants, perfumes, razors, and hairbrushes. His clothes are hung in one area of the closet; her clothes are hung in a different area of the closet. Couples bathe at different times—for the most part. (Bathing together is getting ahead of ourselves. That is a bedroom conversation.)

All other areas of the home are shared, but the bathroom gives you space that is yours alone. The bathroom asks the question, *"How much of my identity is still uniquely me in this shared relationship?"*

Instead of looking at "cases," questions are provided to reveal emotional design, worldviews, and values. If one spouse is a vegetarian for reasons concerning animal rights, and the other loves to eat all kinds of meat, is it necessary for one to ask the other to change his or her conviction and practice? Another example is abortion. Some couples maintain happy marriages despite contrasting views on abortion, while someone else might end a marriage proposal upon realizing his or her view on abortion is not shared. The bathroom helps us clarify and communicate who we are—our values, views, and natural wirings. It is important to love our spouse where and how he or she lives.

Remember you are building a life together, but the bathroom is a great room because there are some things about yourselves that give you your own space. Can you support each other in that space? Happiness and intimacy are still possible *despite* the differences.

The questions in the bathroom give each person a chance to speak about himself or herself. The spouse is not agreeing or disagreeing with the answers, but listening in order to *discover*. The spouse may ask a question for clarity, but not to persuade or challenge a view or position.

Emotional Make-Up

- In what areas of life are you most controlling and why?
- Do you trust others easily, or do people have to earn your trust?
- In what ways are you possessive in relationships?

- Do you have any fears or phobias—heights, flying, certain animals, swimming, or death? What experiences have you had in the past that might have contributed to certain anxieties?
- In the movie *A League of Their Own*, Tom Hanks's character says, "There's no crying in baseball!"[1] Do you see crying or other emotions as a sign of weakness? When was the last time you cried? When is crying a good thing?
- Do you take medication for anything?
- How comfortable are you speaking in public? In what situations would you like your spouse to speak instead of you or for you? In what situations would you like to take the lead?
- What are you sensitive or insecure about? (Perhaps your ability to spell, your body shape, your singing voice, or maybe your lack of athleticism?)
- In what ways might you be jealous or stingy?
- How do you process anger? Is striking another individual ever appropriate or justified? On what occasions have you ever hit anyone?

---

[1] *A League of Their Own*, directed by Penny Marshall, 1992, Columbia Pictures.

- Do you have any unresolved issues with anyone? Has someone taken advantage of you or said untrue things about you? Do those matters need to be addressed? Why or why not?
- Have you ever wronged anyone? Did you ask for forgiveness? If not, why not?
- Is there a childhood experience or a memory that makes you sad to the point of deep regret?
- What typically causes your mood swings?
- How do you cope with sadness, disappointment, or loss?
- What things would you most likely daydream about?
- In what ways are you adventurous?
- In what ways might you express an entrepreneurial spirit? What would you like to pursue though it might have some measure of risk?
- What is the least inviting character trait you possess?
- Should letters or memorabilia of past relationships ever be kept? Might there be good reason or exceptions for keeping these items? Why or why not?
- How freely and to whom do you say, "I love you"? Why?

- What is your favorite picture of yourself and why?
- How important is happiness in your life? What are the things that make you the happiest?
- How important to you is making other people happy?
- What kinds of things encourage your heart the most? (Things like love notes, words of praise, random acts of kindness, and gifts without occasion.)
- Do you have any compulsions, addictions, or noticeable behavioral patterns? (Are you a neat-freak who is relentlessly straightening up, a media socialite who is constantly on Facebook, or an avid reader who always has a book in hand?)

Views and Values

- What is your view of success? How important is it to be successful? What might you sacrifice in order to be successful?
- What laws can be bent but not broken? What standard do you use to differentiate between bent and broken?
- What pattern of behavior do you have that you would like to change?
- What are your most treasured convictions that you never see yourself compromising or changing?

- To what degree are you honest? If a cashier gave you an extra $10 in change, would you drive back to the store to return it? If you found a wallet with $2,000 and contact information inside, would you return the wallet and cash?
- How would you describe your spiritual upbringing?
- What are your current spiritual views of God? Of sin? Of church? Of the Bible? Of Jesus? Of heaven? How does one gain entrance to heaven?
- What spiritual interests do you have, if any? What are your views on astrology, mysticism, angels, and the afterlife?
- Do you have reoccurring dreams? Do you think your dreams mean anything?
- In what ways are you possessive with your possessions?
- Are you prone to ask people for help, or do you see that as an imposition?
- Are you trustworthy? What are the strengths of your trustworthiness and what behaviors do you have that challenge your trustworthiness?

- Do you have any specific views about gender equality? Are there things women do better than men and vice versa?
- Are there things one gender should participate in and the other gender should not?
- What are you views on sexual orientation and gay rights?
- Does sexual behavior possess a moral component? If so, by what standard should morality be measured?
- What is the role of government in your personal life? How much should the government know about individuals?
- According to the Declaration of Independence, the government is to protect one's right to life, liberty, and the pursuit of happiness. What does that mean to you?
- How do feel about guns and gun control? How do you feel about hunting?
- How do you feel about welfare and various forms of public aid provided by the government?
- What is the biggest lie you have ever told? Is lying ever justified? Why or why not?

- What would make your life more comfortable? (Select something that could be put into action rather easily; your answer should not be "to win a million bucks!")
- What is your opinion on the use of therapists for children, marriage, or personal counseling?
- What is the one domestic task you dislike the most?
- In what ways are you different at work than at home?
- How do you see music and the arts as part of your life?
- What books or movies impacted your worldview or brought conviction or awareness in your life?
- If you were going to be an "activist" for some social justice cause, what would it be and why?
- The movie industry uses labels to indicate what is appropriate for viewing audiences. How do *you* define "appropriate" when it pertains to violence, profanity, nudity, drugs and alcohol, respect for authority, and approval of immoral or unethical behavior? When and how are these subjects to be disclosed to and experienced by your children?
- What societal norms offend you the most and why?
- Do you have a personal pet peeve?

- What are acceptable grounds for divorce? Should ground rules for talking about divorce be established?
- What do you think of prenuptial agreements?
- Why do you think some spouses cheat on each other? Define "cheating"?
- What are some "best practices" to help marriages guard against infidelity?
- Talk about the last time you asked someone for forgiveness. What would be some reasons you would refuse to forgive someone?
- Is there anything about your work that your spouse might be ashamed to learn?
- If a serious fight were to occur between you and your mate, would that stay just between the two of you or might you share the situation with a friend or relative?
- Is there anything in your life in which you don't want your spouse to be included?
- In what ways do you combat feelings of prejudice in your life? (If you don't think you are prejudiced in some way about something, think again.)
- What are your views on pornography?

The bathroom allows you to be you. One may vote Republican, and one may vote Democrat. One drinks coffee, and the other drinks hot tea.

If in a premarital relationship, bathroom responses can help a person evaluate the compatibility of the dating relationship. Is this the person with whom enough views and values are sufficiently shared to continue the relationship? Can I love them well, where and how they want to live?

If a couple is married and differences of opinion exist, unconditional love is a necessary resource. Additionally, constructing purposeful bridges when spouses discover they are on different sides of the stream is well worth the time and effort. The building tools in this book will help you.

Do not
disturb!

TEN

Bedroom

Apparently there is regular frustration and disappointment in the bedroom for a lot of couples. The magazine rack at the local grocery store overflows with magazines that run lead articles on having great sex. It might be a women's health magazine, a men's fitness magazine, or just a general lifestyle magazine, but articles abound on "the top ten ways" to pleasure, excite, climax, seduce, arouse, and romance your partner. I saw one article suggesting 101 ways to spice up one's sex life. Man, that's a lot of spice. There are many resources available regarding sexual enrichment. This book may not offer the same kind of coaching typically found in those magazines, but when meaningful conversations about sex occur between couples, their physical intimacy improves. Meaningful conversations will lead you to new areas of sexual fulfillment and help remove hindrances that have kept you from a more satisfying sex life.

The bedroom asks the question, *"How might we be sexually fulfilled?"* If there is perversion, asexuality, or immorality (actual or perceived), these matters should be addressed with a trained therapist. Our focus is on understanding and discovery. Where there is understanding and discovery, happiness and intimacy are more easily realized.

CASE STUDY I

Mary believes she is a normal woman. Max, her husband, does not think so, as it relates to sex. However, Mary has had a few personal conversations with her friends, and her friends share her opinion. For this reason, Mary is pushing back on Max's requests. The couple has been married for three years. Max is twenty-nine, and Mary is thirty-two. This is Mary's first marriage, but Max was married at twenty and divorced at twenty-three. Mary and Max would both say they had a great sex life their first year of marriage, but during the second year, Max started asking more of Mary. There was conversation of role-playing, certain sexual positions, and other "fantasies" that troubled her.

Mary was thoughtful about the matter, and she attempted to be open-minded to his suggestions. However, some of the ideas Max offered made her uncomfortable. When she declined his suggestions, Max rolled his eyes and verbally expressed his disappointment. Since then, the awkward exchanges have often caused tension. This tension contributes to sex occurring less frequently.

One day Max gives Mary a little word of caution. He insinuates that without a healthy sex life marriages don't last. He does not feel that his words were a threat, nor does he feel he was being mean. He was simply being honest. Marriages without sexual intimacy are troubled marriages, and he expects her to respond positively to his suggestions. Mary knows that if she does, she will become bitter and resent him. What are some probable outcomes of this situation? Can you see the concerns each spouse has? What advice would you give them?

Questions:

- In what ways is sex an expression of love and in what ways is sex an expression of lust?
- What dampens your sexual interest? What fuels it?
- Should withholding sex be appropriate at times? If so, when and why?
- What kind of arrangements or agreements should be made if two people have vastly different sex drives?
- Do you consider yourself conservative or risqué as it pertains to sexual fulfillment?
- What other concerns do you observe from this study?

CASE STUDY 2

Trudy was determined to get in shape. "What's the deal?" she thought, as she stood naked in front of her bathroom mirror. "I used to have energy and enjoy running, and my figure turned heads just a few years ago. Now look at me! My breasts are only attractive to a nursing toddler, and keeping up with my four-year-old firstborn is wearing me out!" Trudy had turned thirty-two two months before. The baby weight from her second child was still hanging on a full twelve months after the baby was born. Trudy became determined to find her form and feel good about herself.

Months pass. She started to exercise daily and manage her diet, and she had a little nip and tuck to reclaim the fantastic figure she once had. Now thirty-three, Trudy is fit and beautiful in form and face. Jack, her husband, is very pleased with the results, but there is something that Jack is not pleased with. Trudy has started wearing clothes that greatly accentuate her form. Jack likes her to wear attractive clothing, but lately her choices, to him, mildly resemble hooker-wear. Jack notices that other men are eyeballing his wife. Trudy doesn't mind the attention.

She tells Jack that it is healthy for her self-image, and it is probably healthy for him to be a little jealous. She says, "Jack, during my chubby stage a year ago, your affections were seldom felt. You didn't look at me like you wanted me. I actually felt like I turned you off more than I turned you on. Now that you see what you have you will appreciate it more." Jack tells Trudy not to push him on this issue. He warns that she will not like the outcome. Both are sticking to their guns. A storm is brewing and someone is going to get hurt. What are some possible outcomes of their stances? What would your counsel be to them?

Questions:

- Can you empathize with how each spouse might be feeling in this case study? In what ways?
- How do you feel about your body?
- How important is it for spouses to look pleasing to each other?
- Does it, or will it, discourage you to see your body age with sags and wrinkles? If yes, how do you intend to deal with this discouragement?
- What are your feelings about various forms of plastic surgery?
- What other factors might be present in Trudy and Jack's story?

CASE STUDY 3

Tonya was sitting in the left turn lane waiting for the light to change. An elderly lady approaching in an SUV saw the signal change and proceeded to the turning lane. However, the light change was not for the turning lane, but for traffic proceeding forward. The crash was not at a high speed, but Tonya's resulting spinal injury caused her many years of pain and significantly limited her mobility. She cannot lift anything more than a couple of pounds, and her ability to bend over is impaired. It has been over three years since the accident, and Tonya and her husband Rick have not had sex yet, due to her painful condition. Rick has suggested methods of foreplay and ways to climax, but Tonya has not been open to any of his suggestions.

Rick is understanding and compassionate. He is very caring and concerned about Tonya's condition, but he has normal sexual desires and thinks some of his suggestions could be acted on if she were willing. What are your thoughts, speculations, and ideas about possible options for this couple?

Questions:

- What are the purposes of sex in a relationship?
- Describe the importance and necessity of sex in a relationship.

- Is sex a place where you primarily give or primarily receive?
- How much of sex is physical in nature, and how much is emotional and mental?
- If there were an injury or condition that greatly limited sexual activity with your partner, how would you handle that situation? What feelings would surface in you if you were the one limited? What feelings would surface in you if your partner were limited?

ELEVEN

Attic

My wife keeps things that remind her of sweet past experiences. There is a rocking chair in our attic. She rocked and prayed over each of our children during the wee hours of the night in that chair. I'm not the most tenderhearted guy when it comes to sentimentality. I've wanted to part with the chair a number of times. It has been over twenty years since anyone sat in it. Our kids are grown and out of the house. Other than my wife and me, no one even knows it's there. Therefore, no one else cares. Yet somehow, keeping that chair brings Martha comfort and serenity.

One late evening we reflect on the lives of our children, and Martha begins to share memories. She recalls when she rocked a sick child all night during an extended asthma attack. She mentions a revelation she had while cuddling another child in that rocking chair. She speaks in soft tones as I watch her eyes scroll through time. Her mind gathers memories like a toddler would gently pluck clover, collecting a bouquet of contentment and joy. As she shares her memories with me, the color of her voice shifts like a kaleidoscope, bringing light and depth to life lived, to love given. I love hearing about her special memories of the past. We still have the rocking chair.

Each person has a past. Your past might be very honorable, and you might have many good things to share. People also have experiences they hide and decisions they regret. Both good and bad experiences impact and shape us. What is in your attic? The attic asks, *"What are the experiences of the past that have shaped you?"*

I was once sitting with a couple in their early thirties. They were excited about their wedding ceremony, then just six weeks away. We were finishing the last premarital counseling session and I felt prompted to ask, "Okay—is there a secret of some kind that needs to be shared before rather than after the knot is tied? I'm not trying to bring up bad memories of the past or embarrass anyone, but if there is something you have not shared that needs to be shared before the wedding, be sure and do that soon."

There was a pause in the air. Then the self-employed contractor said, "Well, I've been getting threatening letters from the IRS. I have not paid my self-employment taxes in the last four years, and I think this is all about to come to a head." The young bride-to-be almost fell out of her chair.

Another couple, in their fifth year of marriage, regularly experienced struggle and tension. They had separated twice, and divorce seemed imminent. When I met with the wife, I inquired about her upbringing, and she ultimately disclosed some very painful memories from her childhood. Her mother had abused her in horrific ways. She put those memories "in the attic" and never wanted to talk about them. She didn't want her husband to know of the abuse. It turned out that her husband had a few expressions and innocent behaviors which were similar to those of her mom. This caused her to respond defensively to her husband. With the help of a trained therapist, these issues were addressed, and their marriage was healed and restored.

The attic does not ask that all dirty laundry be aired. There are some things from the past that are not really in the attic. They have been appropriately dealt with and are buried at the bottom of the sea. Do not feel compelled to share stories that only highlight immaturity and silliness, but like the above situations of tax evasion and personal struggles of childhood, share experiences that shape you or will affect you as a couple.

Questions:

- What three childhood experiences impacted you the most? Choose one from fifth grade or before, one from junior high, and one from your high school years. (The events don't necessarily have to be from school.)
- Have you ever been involved in any criminal activities? If so, what were they?
- What kind of driving record do you have? Do you have any DWIs?
- Have you had any traumatic experiences during travel (car, plan, or other)?
- What was the strongest conflict you witnessed in your home growing up? How did that affect you?
- Have you ever been sexually, emotionally, or physically abused? Are you able to elaborate on that experience? Do you still struggle with the effects of those experiences?
- Do you have any outstanding debts, promises, or arrangements that should be disclosed?
- Is there anything immoral or unethical in your past that should be mentioned?
- What else might be in the attic that should come to light?

TWELVE

Back Porch

It was the first time for me to meet this young couple. It was a premarital counseling meeting and it was obvious they were nervous. Her fingers constantly fidgeted. His feet randomly moved to the beat of nothing. It was as if they were meeting with the vice-principal for writing on the bathroom walls. I tried to help them relax. Both carefully answered my questions as correctly and carefully as they knew how. I found it endearing.

When I meet with young nervous couples, sometimes I ask, "What expectations do you have of your future spouse?" The aforementioned young bride-to-be responded with great animation, "Oh, *none!* I trust him to do the right thing. I do not have any expectations of him." I smiled and chalked it up to innocent young love.

I said, "Well, actually, I believe you have a lot of expectations of him." She cocked her head like a curious cocker spaniel. I continued, "Do you expect him to brush his teeth? Do you expect him to have employment? Do you expect him to come home after work, or would it be okay if he hung out at the local bar until two in the morning most nights?"

She said, "Well, no, but he wouldn't do that." She might have been right about her beau. Nevertheless, we all have expectations. Many expectations are fundamentally and silently agreed upon. We see these expectations as common courtesies. These kinds of expectations would be a waste of time to disclose, but there are some expectations worthy of discovery.

Be reminded, this exercise is about understanding and discovery. This is about learning perspectives and ideas. It has *nothing* to do with "right" or "wrong." So when your spouse voices an expectation, and you are surprised or in total disagreement, the best and only response should be, "That's very interesting to me. What makes you think that?" If an explanation is given and you are still surprised by his or her reasoning, simply move on to another question. The temptation might be to say, "That is the dumbest, most self-centered thing I have ever heard!" But then the exercise ceases to be about discovery, and understanding is stymied.

Why is the back porch even in the book? It is because I have had couples tell me that on the back porch they learn a lot about their partners and come to understand things about their relationships that previously confused them.

The back porch represents *the way things should be*, or at least how one sees it in his or her mind. It is Bob and Caroline after a hurried and frantic day, taking a break on the back porch of their Texas Hill Country home. With sweet tea in hand, they pull up the rocking chairs, listen to the birds sing, and feel the tender breeze of an autumn night, and all seems right with the world. It is *the way things should be*. Calm. Perfect. Refreshing. Rewarding. Anxiety-free. Met expectations bring these sensations to us. All of us have "expectations."

For whatever reason, we feel these expectations should be fulfilled to make our world "as it should be."

I had an expectation I brought into my home. I expected my wife to make the school lunches for my children. After all, my mother made my lunch all the years I went to school. It just seemed natural that Martha would make the school lunches for our children. This expectation moved into real time and real life once we were married and had kids. Over time, and after considering the structure and rhythm of our lives, it made sense for me to make the school lunches for our children. Expectations can change. Some *should* change. Some shouldn't. Each person needs to *make room* for possible changes. But here is the point, we have expectations going into the relationship, and the back porch is a safe place to voice them.

I heard one man say to his soon-to-be fiancée, "I love to play golf. I play golf every weekend. If we get married, you need to know that you will be a 'golf widow.' I will be gone a good portion of the day on Saturdays and Sundays, playing golf." This couple married, and sure enough, he kept his word: He played golf every weekend he could. It was good for that expectation to be mentioned.

The challenge of this exercise is that many expectations can be rooted in selfishness. We do not want to foster selfishness on the back porch. We want to uncover it. Sometimes when an expectation is voiced and sits in the open air, a person hears it differently. It didn't sound selfish in one's mind, but once voiced, it seems a little self-centered. The expectation might not be as practical or as important as initially thought, but when it was swirling around in one's head, it seemed acceptable. Some expectations are not selfish, but reasonable, sound, and healthy. These also need to be voiced. The back porch is a great place to practice empathetic listening and dialogue. Let me offer another building tool to use while on the porch.

Differentiation of self

Another very important relational building tool is *differentiation of self*. Differentiation of self is the practice of separating feeling and thought. It is the ability to remain connected in the relationship without having someone else's emotions or behaviors direct one's course. For example, someone's expectations could make his or her partner mad. It would be natural to give a response based on that emotion. Instead, a person should process expectations cognitively.[1]

Consider the golf addict who played golf every Saturday and Sunday. His wife's response could have been, "Why don't you want to be with me on the weekends?" This is a classic emotional response. A cognitive response simply *recognizes* (from re-cognitive, to know again) the premise of the expectation. She now *knows* (and maybe for the first time) that he plans to play golf every weekend. This is good information to know! His desire to play golf does not necessarily mean he lacks desire to be with her. Differentiation of self does not respond emotionally, but seeks to gain accurate information. The back porch is useful because it pursues knowledge and understanding, *not change*.

If there is a topic or situation that is currently bringing tension in the relationship, it is not wise to voice that expectation during the exercise. The purpose of the back porch is to cultivate discovery and understanding. Listen empathetically.

---

[1] Murray Bowen, "Differentiation of Self," retrieved March 16, 2015, from thebowencenter.org.

Additionally, when you voice expectations, voice what you hope to achieve, not what you expect your spouse to do. For example:

Don't say, "I expect you to be home on time so we can have dinner together." This is a pressure statement subtly—or not so subtly—made against your partner.

Instead say, "I expect to have dinner together. It is important, to me, that we share that time together as often and as regularly as possible." The word "you" is not in the statement.

These expectations are things you hope for. The statements are not to be personal demands or digs. You are simply voicing how, in your perfect world, things should be.

Sample Expectations:

- I expect we go to bed together and get up together. To me, it speaks of our unity.
- I expect us to never use the word "divorce."
- I expect that we never spank our children, but use other means of punishment and discipline.
- I expect our relationship to be built on trust and openness to the degree that we open each other's mail and review each other's email.
- I expect to attend graduate school and that each of us sacrifice accordingly to make that happen.

- I expect our household to operate by a followed and agreed-upon budget.
- I expect the niceties we experienced and expressed in our courtship, such as opening my car door, to continue.
- I expect we not take turns on who cares for the crying child in the middle of the night. I expect the one who has the least demanding schedule the following day to take care of the child.
- I expect our children to go to private school.
- I expect an apology when I am wronged.
- I expect we hold hands when we walk through the mall.
- I expect to spend Thanksgiving at my mom's house each year.

Because there is no emotional response on the back porch, there is great liberty to share. There is safety, security, and transparency. And note this: There should be no obligation that any expectation will be agreed upon. Decisions are not made on the back porch, but information is gathered and understanding is gained. The back porch can be extraordinarily meaningful. Each person has opportunity to hear the heart of his or her mate. Such candid comments remove guesswork and assumption. This is extremely valuable as each person processes how to love in the living.

THIRTEEN

The Home's Foundation

I hope you have had meaningful conversations with your beloved as you have gone through this book. I hope you, like Bob and Caroline, had conversations that were initially challenging but, using the correct construction tools, you experienced breakthroughs and new levels of affection and unity. Practicing empathetic listening, regularly choosing dialogue over discussion, and embracing the uniqueness and beauty of your relationship will put you in a good position to experience greater happiness and intimacy.

However, you may have become irritated or disillusioned while discussing some of the case studies or questions.

Maybe you were surprised to learn about some of your partner's values, views, or expectations. There are multiple reasons why couples struggle to be on the same page. Each person has his or her own measuring system for cleanliness, generosity, child-rearing standards, risk tolerance, saving and spending, religious vigor, sense of decency and propriety, integrity, views of faithfulness, friendship, forgiveness, image, sexuality, mood swings, expressions of personality, interest in social justice, dependence and independence, and a host of other values and behavioral patterns. How we process worldviews and express character traits are unique to each person. Couples must learn to move to the music of the home—to love in the rooms in which we live—in order to enjoy the dance. Couples that love and dance well in these rooms experience a happier, more intimate life together.

Is it that simple? After many years of counseling and observing couples, I say, "Yes, it really is that simple."

Is it easy? Not necessarily.

Reflect and Self-Evaluate

A powerful exercise that is often neglected is to simply reflect and self-evaluate. Give considerable thought to these principles. How are you doing?

1. If you want to get closer to your spouse, do you *move* in such a way that helps create connection and convey care?
2. Do you pursue meaningful communication, or do you only exchange factual information or words that express your perspectives?
3. Do you love well by helping your spouse live well?
4. Do you practice empathetic listening?
5. Do you practice dialogue, or do you more often pursue discussion?
6. Do you provide a safe and judgment-free place for transparency?
7. Do you value discovering and understanding your partner more than you value your ways and preferences being followed?
8. Do you embrace and celebrate what makes your relationship beautifully unique?
9. Do you practice differentiation of self?

While moving and responding to our mate in healthy ways is not always easy, it is relationally rewarding and well worth the effort. Moving well creates greater happiness and intimacy. How we move is directly related to our foundation. We mentioned earlier that skyscrapers are built to move. Movement is prepared for in the foundation. It starts there.

This last chapter is about your foundation. Your foundation is what you stand on and what you stand for. In every room you stand on or for something. Your view of entertainment is a stance. Your use of money and view of its purposes is a stance. Your view of friendship is a stance. Your interest in image and reputation is a stance. Your expectation for sexual fulfillment is a stance, and so forth and so on. How you stand . . . the balance and sway, timing and rhythm, and the movement of your feet that compliments your spouse's movement . . . will determine the beauty of the dance. But as we have pointed out, sometimes dancing in a way that compliments your spouse's movement is not easy. Though we are beautifully created, sometimes the moving parts rub together and create friction and conflict; not the graceful movement desired.

In the movie, *The Odd Couple*, Oscar Madison expresses a sentiment to his friend and housemate, Felix Unger. Though Oscar and Felix are not a married couple, the annoyance level expressed by Oscar is classic marriage tension.

> "I can't take it anymore, Felix, I'm cracking up. Everything you do irritates me. And when you're not here, the things I know you're gonna do when you come in irritate me. You leave me little notes on my pillow. Told you 158 times I can't stand little notes on my pillow. 'We're all out of cornflakes. F.U.' Took me three hours to figure out F.U. was Felix Ungar."[1]

It is a funny scene in a funny movie. But being annoyed and frustrated with your partner is not funny in real life. Couples can get on each other's nerves and not see eye-to-eye. It's part of the journey.

Without exception, every couple I know that uses the building tools provided in this book and purposefully connects *loving and living* increases their happiness and intimacy. As stated earlier, some matters should be specifically addressed with professionals. If you are having trouble budgeting your finances, see a financial counselor. If you are struggling with sexual intimacy, make an appointment with a therapist. If raising your kids produces an exorbitant amount of tension, it might serve you well to take a course on parenting. Hearing the rhythm of life, moving appropriately, and practicing differentiation of self is an art. It is not always easy because we all have blinders and blindsides. Therefore, it is helpful to seek

[1] *The Odd Couple*, directed by Gene Saks, 1968, Paramount Pictures.

assistance. Every couple should regularly invest in the health and happiness of their marriage.

It amazes me to encounter so many couples who are discouraged about their marriage, yearning for greater pleasure and affection, *but do virtually nothing about it*. If on the dashboard of the car the engine light turns on, most people investigate the concern and often pay a professional to resolve the issue. Why are couples so resistant in seeking assistance with their marriage when warning lights appear?

Another way people attempt to address a distressed marriage is to "unplug." I admit there is value in getting away from the daily grind. Vacations and retreats are good for body and soul. But trips don't address or solve marital issues. Couples falsely reason that a few days at a quaint Colorado mountain cabin or an all-inclusive Cancun beach resort will rekindle and restore a fractured marriage. Their hope is that the distance and disconnect of the relationship will somehow magically be mended on the slopes or in the surf. Instead, six days and $4,500 later the only thing to show for the time and money spent is a new snowboard or Coppertone tan. But the health and vitality of the marriage pretty much remains the same.

The Third Strand

Two are better than one,
    because they have a good return for their labor:
If either of them falls down,
    one can help the other up.
But pity anyone who falls
    and has no one to help them up.
Also, if two lie down together, they will keep warm.
    But how can one keep warm alone?
Though one may be overpowered,
    two can defend themselves.
A cord of three strands is not quickly broken

Ecclesiastes 4:9–12 (NIV 2011)

Many marriages function with two strands: the husband and wife. And when two people are compatible, understanding, and share similar values and worldviews, a happy marriage with minimum conflict can be achieved. Even still, there is greater strength with the third strand mentioned in the passage above.

The third strand underscores the role God plays in a marriage. When God is brought into a marriage as the third strand, an entirely different perspective comes to life. My marriage is more fulfilling with God as the Third Strand. When He is the conductor, the music is more alluring and pleasant. When He is the instructor, without fail, I am a better dancer and move in unity with my bride with greater ease. The Third Strand helps me listen more empathetically and reveals things to me that my natural mind would not grasp. I am better equipped to love my spouse and help her live well. The result is greater happiness and greater intimacy.

You may be familiar with the story of Jesus' birth as told in the second chapter of Luke's Gospel. Mary and Joseph journey to Bethlehem late in Mary's pregnancy. Shortly after arriving in Bethlehem, it is time for her to give birth to her firstborn child, Jesus. Luke's account says when Jesus was born, Mary "wrapped Him in swaddling clothes, and laid him in a manger; because there was no room for them in the inn" (Luke 2:7, KJV).

We have no information about the inn or the innkeeper. Some have supposed that the innkeeper was grossly insensitive to the situation. Who would turn away a woman about to give birth? Well, we just don't have enough information to rightly judge the situation. The innkeeper may have had limited information, or other factors could be at play. But this we do know: He did not make room. The glory and majesty of God entered the world and the innkeeper missed it because he did not make room.

When I visit with couples experiencing difficulty in their marriage a number of subtle factors are often at work. Most of these couples are usually good people and fairly reasonable. I rarely engage a couple where the husband or wife is a tyrant, mean-spirited, or abusive. Most are simply tired, enduring considerable stress, and lacking affection, attention, and affirmation. This, of course, is the very formula that produces a sense of desperation and emptiness. The Lord, the Third Strand, helps the weary, comforts and calms the disheartened, and infuses a divine love that sustains. Welcome God's presence, the Third Strand, into your marriage.

Make room.

For more information about
the Third Strand, marriage helps,
marriage retreats, resources,
or to order additional copies of *Make Room*,
please visit makeroombook.com

QUESTIONS FOR SMALL GROUPS

Many who read *Make Room* become more self-aware. Or, they experience an "ah-ha" moment. One woman rushed up to me after reading an early version of the book and said with great relief and enthusiasm, "I have my own toothbrush!" (You might recall the bathroom chapter talking about a person's individual identity within the context of a relational union.) This woman struggled with the fact that she and her husband did not see eye-to-eye on everything and it really bothered her. Because there were differences of opinion, she thought something was "wrong" with the relationship. After processing some truths revealed to her in the book, she developed a healthier self-image and became less argumentative with her mate about "little things" they didn't agree on. She said the moment occurred when she "walked" through the bathroom chapter and realized that it was okay to have differences—after all, she had her own toothbrush.

Even though her husband did not read *Make Room*, she benefitted from the content on her own. The book helped their marriage because it helped her.

Another couple told me that one of the case studies fit them exactly. As they talked through the case study using the tools of empathy and dialogue, they began to see the situation in a new light. When they genuinely applied the principle and saw that "loving and living are connected," they had a breakthrough. Each expressed support for the other and the tension they struggled with disappeared. Couples benefit from the book as they process situations in fresh ways and with readjusted lenses and attitudes.

Often, significant learning and "ah-ha" moments happen in community. I have witnessed great transformation in people's lives in a group setting. But I have also seen people abuse and misuse group settings. People can be wounded and relationships adversely affected when group conversations are not directed appropriately.

Because powerful and positive transformation can occur in group settings, I encourage people to make use of the company of good friends whose goal and agreed-upon purpose is to strengthen and encourage one another. We are always better when strength and encouragement are deposited into our lives. But just as you would never put anyone behind the wheel of a car for the first time and say, "Go for it!" before teaching him or her a few essential driving instructions, it is just as important to have some basic instructions on group dynamics. A new driver needs to know where the breaks are located and the importance of stopping at a red light. And a person needs to know some simple rules about group conversation. Otherwise—in both cases—people can get hurt.

If you are going to utilize *Make Room* for group conversation, let's go over a few important ground rules:

1. The most important rule—by far—is to never say anything negative about your partner in the group. Never. Ever.

2. The second-most important rule is to make sure you follow rule number one.

These first two rules seem easy enough to follow, right? But little jabs occasionally sneak in. We might suggest that our spouse is impatient, insensitive, too busy, unappreciative, tuned-out, checked-out, or checking others out. These comments are off-limits in a group setting. If you cannot follow rules one and two you should not review *Make Room* with a group.

These two rules also include questioning your spouse or partner's answers. If your mate shares with the group that he or she has become much more patient after reading the book but you don't think they have become more patient, a group setting is not the time or place to argue the point. If you need to vent or express concerns about the behavior of your spouse, see a counselor. The group is not your counselor nor a place for venting. One of your goals in a group setting is to attempt to make your spouse or partner more appreciated and encouraged than when you arrived. This is a healthy and worthwhile goal.

If you are in a guys group or a ladies group, and you think it's okay to talk negatively about your spouse because he or she is not present, think again. There is no value in making such comments. You would not want negative or derogatory things to be said about you when you are not present.

Make Room group conversations are to trigger new ideas, thoughts, and behaviors that will help you enjoy greater happiness and intimacy with your mate. Conversations within a group setting can help you achieve that. A common approach is to have a dinner party or book club with four, five, or six couples. After dinner, circle up the chairs and spend ninety minutes on the questions below.

Suggested Approach

Whether your group or book club meets once or a half-dozen times to review *Make Room*, any one of the questions below can be used. The questions are in no particular order. The first thing the host wants to do is review the two ground rules mentioned above.

Each person is to disclose what he or she discovered about himself or herself while reading the book. Keep coming back to these central themes:

- Disclosure and discovery of self.
- Posture to learn from others, not judge or challenge.
- Strive to encourage your spouse during group conversation.

Questions:

1. What statement, principle, or author's personal example did you find most interesting in the book? Which was the most helpful? How was it helpful?

2. Which "tool" do you find the easiest to use? Which tool is the most difficult for you to use?

3. Which case study did you enjoy the most and why?

4. What discovery or renewed appreciation do you have for your spouse/partner based on what they shared with you or maybe what you already knew about them?

5 In which room do you hope to see relational vitality increase the most? What specific contribution will you make to help that become reality?

6. How would you score yourself on the nine self-evaluation statements on page 145?
   a. From 1 to 10 (10 being the highest), what would you score yourself before you read the book and what would your score be now?
   b. Which self-evaluation statement, if you applied it regularly, will contribute the most to maintaining health and happiness in your marriage?

7. Is there anything you can do to help your spouse achieve his or her goals or enjoy "living" in a particular room?

8. How do you best express affection and intimacy when you are outside the bedroom? And has your spouse confirmed this expression as a good thing? (Remember when the author led his wife across crowded public places? He thought he was doing her a favor. She felt dragged through the crowd. Be sure you confirm.)

9. In the bathroom there are a number of questions about values and behavioral traits. Did you learn anything about yourself? What value or behavioral trait do you possess that your spouse found cute, encouraging, or admirable?

10. In the last chapter, the author talks about your foundation. Is there a foundation you plan to stand on that is common throughout the house? (This answer could be theme-based. One husband confessed that he needed to "cherish" his spouse more—in every room. Previously, he did not have a full grasp on what that looked like, but now would strive toward that goal and is making progress. He gave examples of how he might cherish her more regularly. One wife expressed her desire to be less nitpicky. She offered examples of what she had become aware of and expressed her

desire to rid herself of this habit.) These theme-based responses are healthy and promising. Additionally, is faith and devotion to God a foundation you stand on? If so, what specific action might you take to help your foundation become stronger?

11. Read the author's commentary on how to "make room" for God on the makeroombook.com website. What are your thoughts?

12. The author noted that we are all builders. We are building a life together. Building is a major theme in the text below:

    > "So then, everyone who hears my words and puts them into practice is like a wise man. He builds his house on the rock. The rain comes down. The water rises. The winds blow and beat against that house. But it does not fall. It is built on the rock. But everyone who hears my words and does not put them into practice is like a foolish man. He builds his house on sand. The rain comes down. The water rises. The winds blow and beat against that house. And it falls with a loud crash" (Matthew 7:24-27, NIrV).

    When applying this text to a marriage relationship, there are some basic truths:

    - Storms are inevitable.

- We all build on something.
- We should all act wisely instead of acting foolishly.

How are these points of application critical in a relationship?

13. Consider three dynamics of marriage that are always present and always in motion: friendship, teamwork, oneness. Each need work and attention.
    a. Friendships are built through shared common interest and activities, which are pleasurable.
    b. Teamwork occurs when things are accomplished. There is a task, an opponent, or an objective. We need the cooperation of team members to accomplish the task, defeat the opponent, or complete the objective.
    c. Oneness is created through a variety of means; learning to speak each other's love language that fuels connection and deepens intimacy.

    Which of the three dynamics need your attention the most right now? Are there specific ways you hope to invest in these areas?

14. If a roving reporter came up to you on the street and asked, "What is your secret to maintaining a thriving relationship with your mate?" what advice would you offer?

15. The principles of the book help us get to a place where we are more transparent, vulnerable, and able to connect on a deeper level. If this is still uncomfortable for you, what is it about you that makes you so guarded? If you are more transparent and vulnerable to your spouse after reading the book than before, what brought about this change?

COLOPHON

Book designed and edited by Kit Sublett for Whitecaps Media. Cover and illustrations created by Kathrine Zeren. Main body and titles composed in Milo Serif OT 11/16, a font designed by Michael Abbink